That Military House

Move it,
organize it
&
`Decorate it`

Written by:
Sandee Payne

Aunt Mary,
Thank you & Enjoy!
♥
Sandee Payne
2006

That Military House: Move it, Organize it & Decorate it
Sandee Payne

First Edition, Paperback
Copyright © 2006 by Sandra B. Payne

Printed in the United States of America
ISBN: 978-1-4116-8780-6

Lulu Enterprises
860 Aviation Parkway
Suite 300
Morrisville, NC 27560

Photography by:
Jennifer L. Bott
&
Red Oak Creative
15 Vassar Road
Audubon, NJ 08106
www.redoakcreative.com

Dedications

For my husband, Michael, who supports my passions, loves me dearly and never minds the changes I am constantly making as I fine-tune our home and our life.

For my children, Corey and Rebecca, who allow their personal spaces to become experiments and for proudly calling every place we live "home".

And for my parents, who have not only passed on their talents, but have kept me believing that I can accomplish anything.

Special Acknowledgements

Many people have encouraged and inspired me to write this book, I would like to thank my friends and clients, for allowing me the opportunity to work on their homes and better their military moving experiences by doing so. To Mary, for always consulting me for decorating advice. To Rachael, for being my soundboard when I had ideas on the mission of this book and to Dara, for listening to me ramble on until its completion, and to all who helped in the editing process.

I would like to also thank the soldiers who make the greatest sacrifice for our country and for those families who make the moves to support them through the years, and still smile…this book is for YOU!

Contents
Introduction

Contents (continued)

You CAN Do-It-Yourself

Painting A Room
Hand-Sewing Basics
Operating a Sewing Machine
Hanging Pictures on a Wall

That's a Wrap

Enjoying your Well-Organized & Well-Decorated Military Home

Appendix A
Inventory Number Grid

Use or Copy this Inventory Number Grid on Delivery Day

Appendix B
Household Inventory Sheets

Use or Copy these Household Inventory Sheets to keep an accurate record of your belongings

Appendix C
About The Author

Get the scoop on the author of
That Military House:
Move it, Organize it & Decorate it
Sandee Payne

Appendix D
References & Resources

Books Referenced
Product Image Resources
Graphic Acknowledgements

Introduction

Being a military family, as you know, has its rewards. You can proudly stand and know you have made a difference in this world; you have dedicated your life to serving your country. You make numerous sacrifices others cannot even begin to understand. You work more hours than you are paid for and relocate your family every few years calling each new duty station "home"…for now. Aside from all the great things you experience, friends you meet and lives you touch, one thing remains unchanged. You are a MILITARY FAMILY.

Your family is your solid ground, your rock, and your safe place in this seemingly unsafe and ever-changing world. So each time you have to pick up and relocate, wouldn't it be nice to have that move happen with ease and excitement, rather than difficulties, chaos and stress? Make this move different from the rest. Learn and apply techniques used in organizing and decorating to make each new house your "home". Make your moving experience enjoyable, something you look forward to, a chance to try out those ideas you have tucked away for your "retirement" home.

Do you ever feel that by the time you get your house just the way you like it, it's time to pack it all up and start again? Well, this book will show you there are time-saving and cost-effective ways to keep your home prepared for a move at a moment's notice, as well as tried and true techniques to unpacking it all and establishing a comfortable home within the first two weeks of receiving your household goods.

This book will walk you through the packing and unpacking challenges, the organizing processes as well as the basic decorating techniques that will change the way you feel about PCSing.

Many questions race through your head once you are notified of a new assignment. Here are some of the common concerns you might experience:

- What type of house will we live in?
- How many closets will it have?
- Will our household goods make it in one piece?
- How many curtains will I have to buy…this time?
- How will the furniture fit?
- What will the storage be like?

Worry no more. It is time to take a different look at PCSing. No longer will PCS stand for your Permanent Change of Station. From now on, within this book, your PCS will be referred to as your Positive Change of Surroundings.

Most interior decorating, organizing and do-it-yourself books provide amazing ideas and beautiful photography. They take your imagination to the extreme and claim to capture the true essence of what your ideal home should look like.

As readers, we take what we can from these works of art and try to make the rooms in our house look like the ones we see displayed. However, it just never seems to look quite right.

Books of that nature are written and photographed by highly educated, talented and obviously resourceful individuals. In order for you to re-create the rooms you see in these books, you would have to invest a lot of time and an even greater amount of money into such involved home redecorating projects.

Have you ever wondered when someone is going to design and publish a book that addresses your decorating and organizing needs as a moving, military family and provide photographs of ideas and concepts that you can actually use in your home, using what you already own? Well here it is, just for you; with the steps laid out in easy-to-follow and easy-to-understand terms. For you, that someone who wants to make changes in your home's appearance but can't envision the ideas to do so.

Use this book as a guide throughout your move to organize and decorate, and 'That Military House' will provide you with a new approach to your home improvement projects; an approach that will leave you with rewarding and enjoyable results. By using this book, you will begin to look at each new home as an opportunity to re-organize your life and your household. You will gain knowledge through your experiences and become creative in your ways of thinking. Some of you may doubt your own capabilities, thinking you are the least creative person you know. Nevertheless, you will soon discover your creative side and others will ask what you have done to get that way.

It all comes down to a few simple concepts:
- ❖ Be prepared
- ❖ Be organized
- ❖ Be clutter-free
- ❖ Be open-minded

Soon you will be ready for any new "home". Enjoy!

Orders in your Hand = Order in your Home

When you are first notified of your relocation, you or your spouse, may or may not, receive orders right away. There are, however, many ways you can prepare for your upcoming move while you wait. Once you receive official orders and your transportation date has been set, only then is it 99% guaranteed that you will be relocating. As your packing date approaches, begin preparing your home for your PCS to ensure the best move possible. Getting your home organized prior to a move can really save you time and energy through the relocation process. By being prepared, your energy can be spent on important issues such as the children and your family.

Important Records and files should be hand-carried from one duty station to the next. In the event of misfortune, you will be sure to have all necessary legal documentation handy, rather than packed away within your household goods somewhere in a warehouse. An accordion file folder can handle the job and is convenient to travel with.

In the check lists that follow, you will find recommended timelines and suggested tasks that can be performed in order for your move to happen more smoothly.

Pre-Move Checklist

Upon receipt of Orders:

❑ <u>*Start a Moving File*</u> for all of your moving related items. Keep in it a copy of your orders, all receipts for moving expenses, travel vouchers, leave forms, claim forms and any other paperwork pertaining to your move.

❑ <u>*Create a Personal file*</u> for each member of the family, in it place the original and a copy of:

- o Birth Certificate
- o Social Security Card
- o Immunization Records
- o Passport
- o ID cards
- o Adoption Records

You can always take them out when needed, but it is advantageous to have them ready well ahead of schedule.

❑ <u>*Set up a Family Records File*</u> for household related and legal paperwork, in it include the original and a copy of:

- o Marriage Certificate/Divorce Papers
- o Insurance Policies (include Company Names and billing addresses, points of contact, policy numbers, telephone numbers and email addresses)
- o Current LES or Leave and Earnings Statement
- o Powers of Attorney/ Original Last Will and Testaments
- o Bank books and account information
- o Previous years Federal Tax Records
- o Vehicle Registrations and Titles
- o Home Deeds and Mortgages
- o Professional licenses and Resumes
- o Investment Information (Account numbers, and other information)

3 *Months* before the Move

- Arrange to visit with the Transportation office to discuss the following issues and dates:
  - ○ Shipment of Household goods
  - ○ Unaccompanied Baggage
  - ○ Pet Shipment
  - ○ Vehicle Shipment
- Request a Sponsor at your next duty station.
- Call the Veterinary Clinic regarding requirements for moving your pet.
- Notify your children's schools of your PCS.
- Check your Credit Report for any outstanding issues or discrepancies; this could affect buying or renting a home at your next location.
- Begin making travel arrangements and book accommodations you will need en-route to your next duty station.

8 *Weeks before the Move*

- ❏ Confirm all dates regarding your move with transportation and the housing office and schedule your pre-inspection.
- ❏ Obtain a floor plan or list of room dimensions from the housing office, landlord or realtor.
- ❏ Design your new room arrangements by using the step-by-step guide to Floor Planning (pgs.17-21).
- ❏ Use up items that can't be moved, like food, cleaning products and other liquids. Try not to purchase additional items until you have used what you have.
- ❏ Make contacts regarding information about your new assignment (i.e. Housing, schools, employment and community services).
- ❏ Check with the housing office at your new duty station regarding advanced application procedures to see if the are accepted. This could put you ahead on the list for government housing.
- ❏ Research your new duty station online, or if possible, visit your new duty station and take photos, pick up maps, brochures and flyers to share with your children.

6 *Weeks before the Move*

- ❑ Begin updating your Household Inventory, or get one started.
- ❑ Decide if you are going to be having a yard sale before your move or after you are settled into your new community. Set these items aside and be sure they are packed separately from your other household goods.
- ❑ Make copies of all your records pertaining to doctors and schools. Notify schools of your upcoming transfer so they can prepare their official records.
- ❑ Obtain a change of address packet from the post office and begin filling out the cards. Contact all creditors, subscriptions and organizations with your new address, and when to make the change.
- ❑ Save all receipts pertaining to your move for tax-exemption purposes. Keep an accurate record in a notebook or computer file.
- ❑ Complete all dental work and exams.
- ❑ Complete all eye care and exams.
- ❑ Obtain a POA, Power of Attorney, from your legal office if necessary. You may need a POA for the following:
  - o Buying and Selling a Home
  - o Shipping or Registering a Vehicle
  - o Shipping your Household Goods
  - o Childcare and Medical Care issues
  - o Termination of Quarters

- ❑ Check with your Homeowners' Insurance provider to arrange transit coverage.
- ❑ Talk to your children about the move. Calm any fears they may have. Show them photos their new house or new school on the Internet.
- ❑ Make arrangements for your pets on airlines; purchase the appropriate travel containers if necessary. Schedule an appointment with the vet for physicals or certificates needed for travel.

4 *Weeks before the Move*

❏ Arrange for storage if you need it.

❏ Begin cleaning and making repairs to any furniture, accessories or other household items. It's better to have projects finished before the move than to put them off until later. There is going to be enough work on the flip side of the move, and these projects will just take a back seat, again.

❏ Hold a yard sale; donate any leftover articles to a local charity. No need to move and unpack household items you have deemed for sale and no longer want.

❏ Launder any linens, sheet sets, curtains and towels that will not be needed in the next month. When clean, fold them neatly and place them in tall kitchen plastic bags with a dryer sheet and tie closed. They will stay fresh and ready for use when your household goods arrive at your new home. This way, the moving company cannot use them as packing materials.

❏ Begin sorting and grouping similar items together. Keep small pieces or matching sets of things together by placing them in zip-lock bags or tying them together with string. Keep the little pieces from toys, games and desk drawers from getting dumped into a box to be sorted upon arrival. Place rubber bands around game boxes.

❏ Update ID cards and Driver's Licenses if needed.

❏ Arrange for Absentee voting ballots if you will be moving during an election.

❏ Continue to speak positively about your move to your family. A positive attitude results in a PCS, Positive Change of Surroundings.

❏ Arrange a date to pick up your child's school records and medications.

❏ Special needs children have additional records that will need to be obtained:
   o Physical or Occupational Therapy Evaluations
   o Current and past IEPs (Individualized Educational Plans)
   o Behavioral and Social Evaluations

3 *Weeks before the Move*

- ❑ Confirm travel arrangements and any temporary lodging reservations.
- ❑ Continue to purge pantry items and non-moveable liquid products.
- ❑ Find a place for everything. If your rooms are not organized when they are packed, the job of unpacking will be ten times more difficult.
- ❑ Follow up on your paperwork and make additional phone calls and contacts to ensure you have the corresponding documents needed.
- ❑ Call your service providers (telephone, cable, internet, oil, electric, water, etc.) and schedule dates for cancellations. Request written confirmation of these dates for your records.
- ❑ Make a list of everyone who needs to know your new address:

  - o Auto Insurance/ Home Owners Insurance/ Renters Insurance
  - o Creditors (Credit Cards, Mortgage Company, auto loans, etc.)
  - o Magazine or Newspaper subscriptions
  - o Doctors and Dentists
  - o Post Office
  - o Department of Motor Vehicles
  - o Banks/ Investors

- ❑ Establish a Bank Account at your new installation.
- ❑ Plan for plants. Plants do not travel well. Give them to your friends as a Thank You. Plants cannot be transported overseas or back to the states when returning from an overseas assignment.
- ❑ Have a "farewell" party for your children. Invite their friends. Let your child help decide to whom he/she would like to say goodbye. We sometimes forget they need closure too.
- ❑ Take a break from the house and plan a short trip. A clear mind is beneficial in the weeks to come.

2 Weeks before the Move

- ❑ Arrange to close any bank accounts you may have opened locally for automated payment services.
- ❑ Cancel any direct deposit or automatic payment arrangements you may have set up with the bank accounts you are closing.
- ❑ Be sure your cars are in good operating condition. Have a 12-point, or similar type of service inspection performed at the local auto body shop or dealer. Have repairs completed before your travel date.
- ❑ Cancel any home deliveries (newspapers, groceries, bottled water, etc.) and arrange for the needed deliveries at your new location.

- ❑ Begin to plan what you will be taking with you through your travels. Set aside toys, books and portable entertainment systems that you will be taking. Be sure you have extra batteries for each item. Launder clothes, gather toiletries and non-perishable food items in suitcases or storage bins.
- ❑ Verify schedules and services with Transportation.
- ❑ Pick up items from the dry cleaners.
- ❑ Weigh your vehicles if you have chosen a partial Do-It-Yourself or 'DITY' move.

1 *Week* before the Move

- ❑ Refill prescriptions. Have enough to cover you through your leave period and travel. Request OTC (over the counter) medications for yourself and your children; pain reliever, fever reducer, cough suppressant, etc.
- ❑ Make arrangements for your children for moving day. Call in those favors from friends that have offered. You will be happy you did.
- ❑ Return all items you have on loan (videos, library books) and remind others to return items they may have borrowed from you.
- ❑ Clean out your refrigerator. Offer these groceries to your friends and neighbors before you throw them away. Have a Party. Use only the ingredients you have left for the recipes!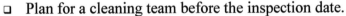
- ❑ Hold aside items you will need to tidy up your house after the movers leave. Arrange to borrow larger items, like brooms, vacuums and tools.
- ❑ Plan for a cleaning team before the inspection date.
- ❑ Take pets for their final check-ups at the clinic.
- ❑ Be sure your luggage is in good working condition.
- ❑ Settle all outstanding bills.
- ❑ Dispose of all flammables properly. Drain fuel from lawn equipment.
- ❑ Obtain traveler's checks for trip expenses.
- ❑ Pick up all medical and dental records. Unless you have power of attorney, the sponsor cannot pick up the records of their spouse.
- ❑ Update and finalize your files for hand carrying. Also include within the file:
  - ▪ Copies of Orders
  - ▪ Emergency Contact information of family or friends
  - ▪ Duplicates of all keys (car, luggage, etc.)
  - ▪ Completed Household Inventory (include photos and videos)
  - ▪ Medical and School records
- ❑ Back up computer files onto an external drive to be hand-carried.

Final Days before the Move

- ❑ Pack your suitcases, travel necessities and snacks. Place all hand-carried documentation aside, either in your car or in a corner of a room and clearly mark them "DO NOT PACK".
- ❑ Collect items you will need handy for moving day and put them in one central location.
  - o Markers, for detailing box contents
  - o Scissors / Utility knife
  - o Trash bags
  - o Pencils and pens, for signing paperwork
  - o Paper towels, paper plates and plastic utensils (for that delivered pizza)
  - o Bottles of water and drinks (a few extras for the movers would be nice)
  - o Hand soap and extra toilet tissue in the bathrooms
- ❑ Dismantle all electronic equipment. Label all wires before you unhook them. This will make setting up your systems easier on the other end of the move. Put all wires in one bag or container.
- ❑ If you have packed any items, do not seal containers. Once sealed, the movers are not responsible for missing or damaged items.
- ❑ Place valuable jewelry or cash in a locked box or fire-proof safe.
- ❑ Separate "professional items" and "unaccompanied baggage".

- ❑ For overseas moves, "unaccompanied baggage" should include light housekeeping items. That can include: iron, dishes, silverware, bedding, clothing and a few toys for the kids.
- ❑ Relax, because you are as ready as you are going to be and tomorrow is going to busy.
- ❑ Get to bed early.

Moving Day

- ❏ When the movers arrive, take them on a walking tour of your home.
- ❏ Point out any items that require special attention when packing or that have original boxes. Also attach a note onto the items with their specific instructions. Make sure you place any original boxes next to the appropriate items.
- ❏ Don't pack anything yourself, let the movers do it. Otherwise, you will be responsible for damage, not them. Guide them if there is a specific way something should be done, but resist the temptation to do it yourself.
- ❏ Point out any items for which you have appraisals (attach a copy of the appraisal to the item). If you can't prove an antique as an antique, then to the moving company it's just old.
- ❏ Show the movers where they can find drinks and snacks. This will keep them from wandering too far when they need to take a break. Let them know if, and what you plan to provide for a meal.
- ❏ Be available to answer any questions as the day goes on.
- ❏ Keep a watchful eye on movers around valuables and trust no one.
- ❏ Before you sign it, read over the Bill of Lading provided to you by the moving company at the time of pick-up. Check to be sure the destination dates and addresses are correct.
- ❏ Before signing the Inventory sheets, look them over very carefully. Take notice of what things they have marked as damaged and be sure to write any disputes you may have on the bottom before you sign.
- ❏ Include a copy of your Household Inventory with the moving company's inventory. It is to your advantage to do this as it may result in a higher claim if a tragedy were to happen.
- ❏ Use a marker or pen to itemize what goes into each box as they are packing. For example, expand on 'Kitchen Items' with silverware, blender, dishtowels, etc.

After the Movers Leave:

- ❏ Have a Clean-Up Party with your friends. You provide the cleaning products and food, and they provide the labor. Your house will be clean and ready for your 'final out' in no time.
- ❏ Turn off all appliances and the water, open the fridge and freezer doors.
- ❏ Inspect the attic, basement and garage for things that may have been overlooked and left behind.
- ❏ Box them up and mail them to your new address. Save the receipts so you can claim the postage.

After you arrive at your new Duty Station:

- ❏ Immediately notify the Transportation Office. They will in turn get in contact with the moving company to arrange the date for delivery of your household goods.
- ❏ Get started on filing your travel voucher. It is possible to need more than one, depending on how you moved.
- ❏ Organize all of your travel receipts and other documents that might be needed sooner than later.
- ❏ Begin preparing any claims for your household goods.

FLOOR PLANNING

How many times do you look at a room in your house and know that it doesn't look the way you would like it to, but you just don't know how to fix it? How many times have you re-arranged that room and still cannot seem to get it right?

One of two things has happened here. Either you have made the most common mistakes in decorating and lined your furniture against the walls, with all pieces side by side, attempting to open up the room, or you have gotten stuck in a rut with placing your furniture in the same pattern in every house you have lived regardless of the architectural details of the room like doorways and windows.

Let's discuss the first scenario using the living room as our example. Small rooms can actually appear even smaller, and large rooms can appear too large if you line items against the walls. You have to create a balance between the actual size of the room and the size you want the room to appear.

By lining the furniture around the walls in almost a circular pattern, with the coffee table in the center, you have created a very uncomfortable and awkward living arrangement. The function of the space has also been disrupted by the traffic flow passing throughout the room. Visitors will have to yell at one another to be heard. Maybe that was acceptable back in the ice age when everyone took their 'chair' and gathered around a fire, but hopefully you have come out from the cold and have moved forward in time. It makes perfect sense that the coffee table would belong in the center of the conversation area so everyone can utilize it for his or her glass. It can also be a nice focal point for a decorative object.

You have to consider a few things before you push your furniture too far. It creates a much better look if your sofa and chairs are away from the walls and closer together, with the table in the center, creating a more intimate feeling. A small area rug under the coffee table would define that zone nicely. Be sure that everyone seated in that space can be seen and heard easily.

Enter the room from every doorway and walk around the room. The conversational area should not be disrupted. If you must walk in front of the sofa to get from the front door into the kitchen, than the area you have created is not the best option. Move the pieces around, keeping them together, until you find the space that will be just right. Keep the sofa away from the walls about 3 feet. This will allow people to easily walk behind the conversational area rather than through it. The room should invite you to enter and move throughout, not become a barrier and stop your guests dead at the doorway. Use the largest wall to begin the placement. If you have a large wall unit or a fireplace, the space in front of it should not be blocked by the back of a sofa. Keep the space clear. As you enter a room, you should not be looking at the back of any furniture. If you are forced into this situation as being the best layout for your room, place a small trunk, sofa table or bookshelf against the back of the sofa to break up the large blank surface area.

Once this conversational area is established, you can add other furnishings (i.e. cabinets, units, plants, floor lamps, end tables and accents). If the main focus and purpose of the living room is to view the television or admire the fire, then be sure every seat is a good one. Avoid creating that circular pattern around the TV.

Approach every room in the house with the same frame of mind. Don't be discouraged if you find yourself making small changes. It takes even the best decorators a few tries before they get it right. You have to live in, function in and admire your space.

A helpful method to developing your room layout is to use a grid floor plan ahead of time. Whether you are moving into government quarters or renting/buying a house, there is usually access to a home's blueprints or floor plans. Obtaining a copy of these plans from the landlord, realtor, the housing office or Internet website enables you to get a head start on moving in, organizing and decorating your new "home". Many of these sites list the room dimensions as well. Although you may not know the exact placement of the doors and windows, based on the details provided in the plan, you will be able to determine which pieces of furniture will fit best in which rooms.

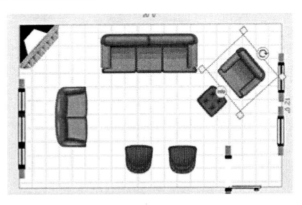

When you gain access to the dimensions of your spaces it is easy to set up the rooms by creating your own paper floor plan. There are many Internet sites and software programs that can assist you in building and designing the best plan for your room. These programs do take time to learn, require practice and can be rather costly. The fastest and most economical way to accomplish what those programs set out to do is the "snail-mail" method, using good ole' pencil, paper and scissors. It is actually fast, easy and fun. Let me show you how to apply this method:

Tools Needed:
- Graph or grid-lined paper
- Scissors
- Pencil
- Scotch tape (optional)
- Measuring tape
- Plastic page protectors
- 3-ring binder

You are going to be making puzzle pieces of all the major pieces of furniture and accessories in the house or room and rearranging them on the graph paper until you discover which placement works best. It's as easy as that!

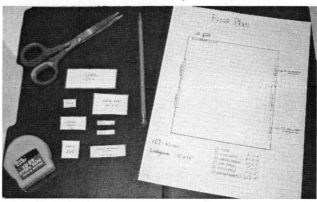

Steps to making a floor plan:

- ❖ Use the measuring tape to measure the floor space of the room.
- ❖ Mark the dimensions of the room onto one sheet of the graph paper. Of course the paper is smaller than the actual room, so let's say, as a recommendation, 1 grid square will equal 6 inches.
- ❖ Measure the large pieces of furniture and draw the outline dimensions on a separate piece of graph paper applying the same scale of 1 grid square= 6".
- ❖ Write the name and measurement of the items in the box you just outlined (i.e. Sofa 6'L x 3'D).
- ❖ Continue this process until all the furnishings in the room have been measured and represented on the paper. If an item is round, measure the widest points and note it in the box. No need to measure smaller accent items like pillows and lamps. Just focus first on the main pieces of furniture and items that take up floor space.

❖ Cut out all the shapes of furniture. If they represent a round object, and you feel especially talented, cut the circles into circles and the ovals into ovals.

❖ Now you can use the floor plan and the cut out pieces to determine what will be the best arrangement for the room.

❖ Once you decide the best layout, you can temporarily tape down the items and slide the finished floor plan into a clear plastic sleeve and keep it in a binder labeled 'Home Floor Plans'.

❖ Prior to your household goods being delivered at your new duty station, remove the sleeves of floor plans and tape them to the walls in the appropriate rooms. This will assist anyone who is helping you and the delivery crew to place your large furniture pieces in the assigned positions.

Your 'Household Inventory' is a very crucial part of your military moving experience. It is a concise and detailed list of everything you own. If you already have an inventory in place, prior to a move, this is the perfect time to check and see if it is up to date. Many of us have good intentions when we get married or move out on our own to start such an inventory. As time passes, and we start to accumulate many new items, we have a tendency to, not only forget to update it, but to forget about it all together.

It is advisable to update your household inventory once a year. Choose a time in the year when you can remember to do it. A suggestion would be to do it at the same time you are preparing to submit your yearly federal income taxes? Files and receipts, etc. are already out. Save yourself a lot of work by doing it then, rather than getting it all out again at a later time. Keep it updated with the correct costs and purchase dates, and then either file or discard the receipts. When processing a claim for an item that is valued or purchased for over $100, it is very beneficial to have kept your sales receipt.

If you do not have an established inventory, before or after a move is an ideal time to start one. There are many web sites that can provide general ideas to get started on creating your inventory and others that provide printable full-page templates. Check with your homeowners' or renters' insurance company. They usually have a basic pamphlet to get the most important and most valuable of possessions documented. If you are computer program savvy, there are a variety of software programs available too. Just remember to back up your file by copying it to a disk or thumb drive and then hand-carry it to your new location. If these files are only saved on your computer's hard drive, and your computer is damaged, gets lost or goes missing, you will not have a complete list of your household goods. It is better to be extra safe than extra sorry.

The following is a list of the necessary or preferred information that you should have on each item list:

- Item
- Description (Mfr./Brand & Serial/Model No.)
- Purchase Date
- Original Cost

If you do not have all of the above listed information, fill it in as best and complete as possible. Having the items listed is most important. Once you become familiar with what you should have on file, you will be able to add additional information as you acquire new things.

If you decide to print out an inventory template or worksheet, leave it blank when you print. It is best to fill all the spaces with pencil. As things change, it is

easiest to erase a line and re-write it in than it is to get on the computer and re-print a new page. A one or two inch 3-ring binder with clear page protectors will keep the pages organized. This will also give you a built-in pocket to keep things such as receipts, warrantees and instructions. For example, in the page titled 'Kitchen', the pocket should have all related items for furniture, dishes, appraised collections that you have in that room. A room-by-room inventory makes it easier to find the needed item. Attach a few photos of the room and a close-up shot of any valuable items to the inventory sheet.

When you are redecorating or remodeling, you will most likely be working in one room at a time. Collections and high value items for which you have professional appraisal documentation can be kept on an additional list at the end of your inventory if you feel the need.

In addition to writing your inventory, there are other ways to document your household goods. A video inventory with narration or a digital photo inventory is a great thing to have to help with identifying replacements or filing a difficult claim. I still highly stress the need for the written version. When the occasion for relocation arises, make a photocopy of the inventory pages and attach them to the 'outbound' inventory sheets. Take this as a wise, but not mandatory, piece of advice. Your records will prove much more valuable in the event of a missing box or crate.

Most often, the description of an item or a box's contents, on the inventory sheet, is rather vague. It is very common for a box full of kitchen appliances, serving pieces, cookbooks, dish towels and candle votives to be recorded by the moving company as 'kitchen items'. The packers are working quickly and do not have the time to list every item individually. Therefore, they generalize and write a brief description based on the majority of what they put into each box. By having a detailed list of your household items, you will be able to identify every item that you own.

The following is a sample of what an inventory record should include:

Room: *Kitchen*

Item	Make	Model	Purchase Date	Cost	Receipt/Warrantee
Microwave oven	*LG*	*A1234*	*1/15/1998*	*$99*	*Y*
Blender	*Kitchen Aide*	*b234*	*2/30/2001*	*$159*	*Y*
Pots and Pans	*Calphalon*	*Cp02*	*Jun-00*	*$450*	*N*

Use the pages in Appendix B (pgs. 225-232) to establish your Household Inventory. You can also photo copy them or prepare pages on your own to get started on your Household Inventory. (Use a PENCIL, so you can make changes!)

<u>Notes</u>

Another Home, Another Chance

At this moment, you are holding the 'keys' to your new military home. Unlock the door and step inside with confidence. You will be tackling the feat of unpacking and settling into your new environment and community. Before you jump in with both feet, as you may have done in the past, there is some planning to do.

This move will be different from all others. It is a new beginning. When you use your resources and apply the knowledge you have attained as a transient military member or family, you will begin to understand your PCS, your Positive Change of Surroundings.

Let us begin with your LES. As you know it, a Leave and Earnings Statement shows that, as a military member, you are living on a limited budget. You have learned to use your money wisely and have made numerous sacrifices to have your money go far. Now we can look at the LES of your move. You must Learn to Evaluate your financial Situation. Your 'situation' can be that of many things. It may be the amount of BAH or Basic Allowance for Housing you will receive the size of your home, the limited storage space available, the damage done by the moving company or how much extra cash will need to go into establishing your family and your home, again.

Along with your own concerns about relocating your family, there are many additional factors that should be considered when choosing your new home. You need to evaluate the pros and cons of accepting government quarters versus renting or buying a home. Above the BAH, there are financial obligations to any new home that may alter your spending budget. Discuss the following with your spouse, and try to take into consideration all family member needs.

- How long is the commute? Consider the price of gas.
- What are the utility features? Oil vs. Electric vs. Gas, and what are their average costs? Ask the realtor or landlord, call the utility company to find out these values and add them into your budget plan.
- Will you use a realtor to find a home? Or search the classified ads?
- What is the school transportation for the children? Can they walk, take the bus or do they need to be driven?
- Will you apply for a VA loan? How much do you need?
- What is the square footage of the home? Will it accommodate your household goods or will you need to pay for additional storage?
- Is there repair work that needs to be completed? What will the cost be to have these done?

Once you decide if you are moving into government housing, a rental property or buying a home, the next steps apply to all. You assume there was some form of an inspection at the time the last residents moved out, but this usually leaves

a few areas untouched and overlooked. Possibly, the walls need to be repainted, or they are freshly painted white. Maybe the carpets are not your style or there are no carpets at all. In most cases, there are going to be things you want to have different from they way they are. Let this be to your advantage.

Use this opportunity to visualize your new home as a blank canvas. Let your mind 'see' your home, as you would like it to look in its final stages. No boxes, organized, ready to be lived in. This is an important step in creating your new home. Visualizing your belongings in their ideal places is your first challenge. Before your household goods arrive, make decisions about permanent changes, such as paint and carpeting. Consider the pros and cons to each change. It is much easier to make big adjustments before your rooms become full. You must have an idea of what you want, think it through, allow for it in your budget and then act on your decision.

All of these steps should be well thought-out before you rush into buying things you 'think' you need only to find yourself in line with returns later. Impulsive shopping and hasty judgment causes unnecessary spending.

Maybe you consider yourself the type of person who has become trapped into ordering custom-sized carpets or draperies to fit odd-shaped rooms and windows every time you move. As you are unpacking your curtains again, take a mental inventory of what you have. How many of these products were bought on impulse? How many are custom shapes and sizes? How many will just not work again because, so far, no two homes have been the same?

Naturally you would put them back into the box and off to the store you drive. Realize that if you are having a hard time with your space, there undoubtedly have been many others here before you that have felt the same way.

Do not make the mistake of 'custom' shopping again. Put away your keys and forget about the shops, for now. Purchasing ANYTHING made to custom fit into military quarters is a serious waste of money, time and resources. Spending your hard-earned pay on something not guaranteed to fit EVERY home you live in is wasteful. Now apply this same concept as you tackle the other areas of your home; the furniture, dishes, linens and toys.

When the time comes for you to make those necessary purchases, make sure you check out the discount shops like TJMaxx®, Marshall's® and Home Goods®. As advertised, they sell brand names for less, and that's no joke! Don't forget about purchasing slightly used items. Especially when you are in the market for your accent pieces, there are some great bargains to be had at flea markets and tag sales. Can't find what you're looking for in the thrift shops or second-hand stores? Read on and you will find that there are many ways to achieve the look you desire by using things you already have in a more non-traditional fashion. You will also learn, or be reminded how to make wise spending decisions when you actually must make those important purchases.

Remember that we are dealing with your new PCS, your Positive …keyword here…Change of Surroundings. Now that you are starting to understand how going 'custom' and being an impulsive shopper can be an impractical way to spend money and time, let's focus on the alternatives that may save you loads of cash and numerous hours of work.

By using the resources available to military members and families, you can acquire the assistance you need and the items you want without breaking the bank. Turn to your new neighboring community. If you are moving in, it is without a doubt there are families moving out. Perhaps they have made the previous error of making custom purchases.

Many times others have already made the mistake of spending before evaluating their PCS, of thinking in the present instead of in the future. They most likely will be more than happy to make a deal with you, one that is much better, and less expensive than a new purchase would cost. You never know, they may just have those custom mini-blinds you were looking for. Keep your eyes open as you are getting to know your new community. Frequently, flyers are posted on bulletin boards around the installation that list items for sale by others.

Almost every military installation has a Thrift Shop where household items are available for purchase at a fraction of the cost of buying them new. These items vary from mini-blinds, appliances (great resource for those 220V needs), draperies and carpets (choose only if they came from a smoke-free home where no pets were owned). The nice thing about a Thrift Shop is a percentage of your cost is recycled into other organizations on the installation. Therefore, you are not only helping someone by buying their no longer needed item, you are also helping build funds for your installation. Keep the Thrift Shop in mind when you are in the process of cleaning out what you own. Think of how you can help others like yourself, who may need what you do not. As the phrase goes, "One's trash is another's treasure." As you take this moving experience one small step at a time, this and other money-saving methods will be brought to your attention.

Lastly, you can always rely on your installation's DIY store for your hardware and home repair needs. Military installations have resources available to you that you may be  unaware of. The name varies from place to place, but it's usually called the Do-It-Yourself, or DIY store. These stores have one purpose... that purpose is to provide you with hundreds of items to assist you in maintaining the appearance and function of your home or government quarters. Every installation has its own rules pertaining to user privileges. If you reside in assigned government quarters you are most likely allowed this service. Military members choosing to live in approved government rental homes, private rental homes or personally owned homes should inquire with the housing office prior to visiting the DIY facility. Once approved, you can easily acquire a user-card by attending a brief session on the guidelines of the facility and immediately begin "shopping". Household items that are usually available include light bulbs, paint and supplies, screws, hooks, shower and tub fixtures, just to name a few. When a home improvement project requires the use of tools or equipment that you do not own, they may have them available for you by signing these items out 'on loan' or by paying a minimal rental fee (I.e. for woodworking, power washing and carpet cleaning).

There are many of you who have never stepped foot in such a store, possibly mislead by what it was. Checking out your DIY store first can save time and money. If the problem is other than electrical or plumbing (call in a DPW work order for these), you can usually fix it yourself with just a little DIY assistance.

You should now be finding yourself a little more prepared and somewhat excited about creating your new 'home'.

<u>Notes</u>

Delivery Day

The alarm goes off... it's early...about 5:30am...you get up and start the coffee while you wait for the delivery of your household goods...and you wait...and wait...Take a deep breath, enjoy these last few minutes of silence and relaxation. You are about to embark on a journey of a lifetime. You are going to discover a whole new world of moving, organizing and decorating 'That Military House' of yours. Be open-minded and confident about yourself and your ability to succeed in making this PCS easy and pleasant for the entire family.

This is the day we all look forward to time after time. You are so anxious to get your new home together and start enjoying your new duty station, or assignment. The next few days are going to be busy. You may be exhausted from your traveling adventure, over-whelmed by all of the new home preparations and tired of sleeping in the guest quarters, hotel rooms or on the floor of your new home.

Well, the wait is finally over. Possibly you have already made a few friends who are willing to help you as the truck unloads your household goods. If not, do not panic, you can do it alone with a little organization and some prioritization. Have the following list of items handy in a basket or small box placed in an area that will be the center point for everyone involved in the move–in process.

- Pens and Markers
- Pads of paper
- Scissors or a utility knife
- Screwdrivers (flathead and Phillips)

In addition, offer the movers fresh water. Individual sized bottles are preferred and the temperature of this water should not be too cold. The job they have is a very labor intensive. Imagine yourself walking the treadmill and stairs for hours while bending and carrying heavy boxes. Water is very refreshing and will help them stay hydrated so they can work more efficiently. Sodas and sugary juices will provide them with an initial burst of energy but may then cause them to tire more quickly, possibly resulting in an extra long day and many needed breaks.

The most important job of the entire day is to have someone responsible designated as the inventory number-checker-offer. The task of this person is to be the first line of communication with the delivery crew to cross-reference the inventory numbers from the boxes and items with the numbers on the inventory sheets.

As the inventory numbers are called out, check off the corresponding numbers on your inventory sheets or on the number grid. Usually provided by the moving company, this one page grid will expedite the process and eliminate the need to continuously flip through multiple pages. When you place the call to verify the delivery date of your household goods, ask if the particular company provides such a grid sheet. Using graph paper or an Excel spreadsheet, you can create your own number grid with the exact count of inventory numbers according to your moving inventory sheets. Separate each group of one hundred by leaving one row blank. (I have provided one for you in Appendix A, pg. 223) This will make finding each number easier at the time of delivery. If for any reason you feel the need to change the way the process is happening, speak up immediately. Be sure the numbers are being called clearly and slowly. Missing a number can cause needless work later. Don't be afraid to ask them to repeat themselves. In most cases there are several people unloading and several numbers being called out the same time.

If you are by yourself and are not sure what to do or where to be, it is best to locate yourself either at the truck or at the door where your boxes will be brought inside. By labeling the rooms with signs ahead of time, the movers will appreciate the effortlessness of only having to carry each box one time. Once the truck is unloaded completely, and every inventory number has been accounted for, you can have the workers move boxes and other things, like heavy furniture, into more desirable locations within the room, if necessary.

Let the movers handle the boxes and other items. They are responsible for any damage that may happen while they are at your house If you take over, they are not responsible for any claims you may submit later. It is tempting to help out by unloading or carrying things to their proper places. Try to let the movers do their job, and you do yours.

Be sure to note any external damage to any boxes or items that are unwrapped by the carrier or damaged as they are unloaded. These items will need to be written on the carrier's claim sheet, **DD Form 1840**, before they drive away.

There are additional jobs for other people that have volunteered to help you. One person can be located at the main door, where all the boxes will be brought in, to guide the carriers to a designated room or area of the house. Let them know if the boxes go to the attic, garage, basement, etc. This will save you a lot of energy at the end of the day. The movers are being paid to be there for you; use them to get things into the right parts of the house.

Many boxes and wrapped items contain only a single article. Others assisting you in your move can open the boxes that contain lampshades or pillows. Wardrobe boxes containing clothing still on the hangers can be opened and emptied right into the closets. Locate the boxes that contain your towels and bedding provisions. Having them unpacked and ready in their suitable rooms will do away with the need to hunt for them when the day is through and you are ready to go to sleep. Clothes can be unpacked and put into drawers and further linens can be put into closets. These larger boxes can be broken down or filled with packing paper and given right back to the movers. They can take them away at the end of the day, freeing up floor space essential for the more tedious tasks of unpacking boxes and finding places for all your belongings.

When it is time for lunch, ask someone to make a run out for sandwiches or pizza and cold drinks. Let the movers know early in the day if you will be providing them with a meal, this will allow them to plan their breaks accordingly. By keeping the movers well provided for with food and water, they will not be tempted to drive off for a long lunch.

Children can often feel neglected and over-whelmed by the whole moving experience, but don't forget that this is their move too. If they express the desire to help out, let them. By creating the signs or posters to label the doors and rooms, they will feel they are important and an integral part in making the move a success. They can also sell lemonade on the curb or visit with friends you may know from a past assignment. If you are new to the community and have yet to make friends, it is important that you have a plan ahead of time for your children. Locate your community recreation center for programs or services that will be available during the dates of your move-in. Make it a priority to register your child or children with the Child Development Center. If they have hourly care vacant, sign up. In the end, the best place for the little ones is where they are happiest and where they are not under you or in the way of the carriers.

Furniture that was disassembled in order to be moved should be reassembled by the movers. This service is normally printed in the transportation contract. Have them assist you in putting together beds, shelving units and large furniture pieces. They may offer to unpack all of your boxes. Although this may sound tempting, allowing this to happen is going to leave you with loads and heaps of stuff everywhere. There will be piles of books and toys on the floor and piles of dishes and glassware covering countertops and tables, leaving you no room to maneuver and no way of telling what item came out of what box, which can be important if you will be needing to file a claim.

As the last box is unloaded and joins the others placed all over your house, your personal space will seem to close in around you. It may seem as if it will take you months to settle in. Nevertheless, you want to make your house your home, and you want to do it quickly and efficiently.

So, you dive into the boxes and start pulling things out, just eager to get the boxes out of the house and onto the curb. Well, **STOP**! This may seem like the most reasonable approach in getting through it all at that very moment, but let's explore a more productive method.

There are typically two ways to go about unpacking. First is the 'make a bunch of piles and get rid of the boxes' way just mentioned, and then there is the 'one box at a time way', or what I referred to as the '**3-box-method**' of organizing. This can be done very easily and is best done either as you are unloading the boxes for the first time, or as you are finding places to put your belongings. Set aside an area in each room for this process.

Here is a basic outline of this method:
- Find three empty bags or boxes.
- Label these boxes: **Keep, Sell/Donate** and **Discard**.

- In the box labeled **Keep** place:
  - ✓ Items you use regularly
  - ✓ Gifts and mementoes that you display and enjoy using
  - ✓ Favorite articles of clothing that fit and are up-to-date

- In the box labeled **Sell/Donate** place:
  - ✓ Items you never use that are still in good condition
  - ✓ Clothing that no longer fits but is still in style
  - ✓ Duplicate household items
  - ✓ Home décor items you have replaced with new ones
  - ✓ Electronics that work and are compatible with the present technology

- In the box labeled **Discard** place:
  - ✓ All broken or damaged items beyond repair
  - ✓ Worn or dated clothing and linens
  - ✓ Electronics that have been superseded by new advances in technology
  - ✓ Paperwork not needed for federal tax filing (i.e. notes, greeting cards, receipts, etc.)

These categories will be found throughout each chapter, to guide you through the '**3-box-method**' of organizing including more room-specific issues, items and processes.

While you are reading on, pick up the telephone and order that last take-out meal. By now you are sick of Pizza and Chinese food, but make this time your last Hoorah and go out with a bang. You have more important things to do than go crazy in the kitchen looking through boxes for your pots and pans and scrounging through cabinets trying to find a few food items you may have left from the guest quarters or hotel that will make a decent meal.

That being said, you should be eager to try the '**3-box-method**', and here is why.

1. Everything will have a place other than on the floor.
2. Your claim, if required, will be practically finished when the last empty box hits the curb.
3. You will be amazed at how fast your house is put together and how good it looks.

Take time to get prepared. Do not open a single box until you have a pad of paper ready to jot down any damaged items and their inventory number from the sticker on the box. If there is more than one person helping unpack, be sure there is paper handy for each of them. This time-saving step needs to be completed at this moment; otherwise it becomes a daunting task trying to figure out which box each damaged item came from after you have disposed of them. Actually, come to think of it, that becomes an impossible task.

A great place to start unpacking is in the kitchen. Dish-pack boxes are very heavy because of their 3-ply density and usually are jam-packed with smaller and more fragile items like glasses and place settings as well as heavy pots, pans, casserole dishes and appliances. With the kitchen cleared of boxes and packing materials, you can be on your way to providing your family with nutritious meals and will no longer have to indulge in take-out three times a day. The heart of a family is in the kitchen, it is impossible to go through an entire day without the use of it. Once your family can function in the kitchen, you will begin to feel like you are really 'home'.

The second most important room or rooms to unpack are those of your children. In preparation for the move you may have discussed changes that would take place when you got to your new home. Possibly a toddler will be moving up to a twin size bed, or there will no longer be training pants at the "new house". Maybe you have even planned major changes like a whole new color scheme or have bought a complete set of fresh bedding. Whatever the case may be, your child has been waiting for the day when they will be reunited with their toys and personal belongings. Keep your child excited about being in a new place. Let them help out when it comes to unpacking their room. The sooner they get their space together, the sooner they feel established.

When you begin to unpack each box and unwrap each item, observe it closely. If there is anything wrong with it, that wasn't wrong before, write it down. Include on your list the inventory number from the box and any damage you notice right away. You can get a more detailed look later, but keep good notes now so you know what to go back to. You can even make annotations regarding when you received it, whether it was a gift, where it was purchased and its cost, if you remember. Place any damaged items aside so they do not get forgotten. After the box is emptied and you have examined its contents carefully, not forgetting to check all the paper balled up in the bottom, you can discard the box. When the last box is discarded, you should have a complete list of items needed for your claim and everything should be in its place. Submitting your insurance claim can financially help you replace or repair those items that are not in the same condition as they were in when they were packed.

You may be the type who cannot be bothered. You figure you have 30-90 days before you have to turn on your claim so why complete it now. You assume all the damaged items are minor and too little to worry about.

Possibly the time it will take you to sit down and fill out all the paper work is just not worth it. Well, no claim is too small. All those little things add up and we are talking about your personal things here; a gift you received for your wedding, a special token of friendship from someone you knew at your last duty station, an heirloom piece of furniture or jewelry from your family. These possessions are valuable in their own way…and they were not damaged before you packed them.

Moving your entire household sets you up for the ideal time to "clean out the closet" and get rid of the things you no longer use, never liked in the first place, and have grown tired of. Taking the extra time to sort these things out while you are unpacking everything, can be very productive.

Although this probably doesn't seem to you like the best time to start a project of cleaning out (hello… I just moved here!), rest assured you will notice quickly that this is the best if not only time to clean out and to do it well. Think back to how many times you say, "We have got to clean out!" Guessing that number is high and that phrase is said almost weekly, this seems like the perfect time. The time it will take now is minimal in comparison to doing it later. When else do you get the opportunity to clean out the whole house? Not just a closet or two at a time, we're talking the WHOLE house.

There is a standard rule of thumb when making the decision to keep or get rid of your belongings. The rule states that if you have not used it in the past year…you won't use it again. The reason the time period is one year is that this allows you to go through all the occasions, seasons and holidays once. Believe it or not, people have a tendency to pull out and use the same favorites time and time again, leaving those not-so-favorites for 'next time'. However, as military families, we are given a bit of a longer grace period. Each new assignment brings with it new climates, new activities and new needs. It would be a shame to throw away your snow boots while you are stationed in the sunny south, just to be stationed next time in the snowy north. Consider these possibilities when you are sorting through your bits and pieces. As you are emptying each box, immediately make the decision as to which of the three boxes in the '**3-box-method**' it will go into. If you put this off, you will never find the time later, and those things that are sitting on the shelves and filling your closets will be there to stay.

When the box labeled '**Keep**' is full, find a place for each item and put it where it belongs. As the other two boxes fill, take the box labeled '**Discard**' outside to the curb. In addition, take the '**Sell/Donate**' box to the garage, basement or storage area and close it up. Do not look in it again. Later you can go through and distinguish between which items are for donation and which are for sale, but not until you have completed the task of emptying every box in every room in the exact same manner.

Unless you are into having yard sales or enjoy making those trips to the Thrift Shop, I would suggest you limit the amount of items in the sell box. By being prepared ahead of time, a yard sale can be a good money-maker.

As mentioned before, the Thrift Shop is a great place to donate and sell. Look into your community or installation thrift shop to see what the fast moving items are. The volunteers there can also advise you regarding which items are best for consignment and seem to be what other people are looking for.

 Charity organizations such as The Salvation Army and Good Will are usually more than happy to take donations. Remember to have the organization fill out a charitable donation form that shows the approximate value of the items donated. This is necessary and beneficial to have if you itemize your Federal Tax Return.

It must be noted here, that a child's room deserves a little special attention during the move-in phase. When you are unpacking your child's room, you can choose to have your child help you or not. An older child can sometimes be reasoned with into letting go of toys they do not play with and clothes they no longer wear. They can help determine what their favorites are and can participate in a big way when it comes to organizing their own space. Use the '**3-box-method**' of organizing for them too. They will actually wind up doing a better job than you ever could. This does not always hold true for the little ones. These material possessions are the only things that have not changed for them during this moving process. It is all of their "stuff" that makes them okay about moving.

Although a teenager's main concerns are about their new home or their new school; a young child may be more worried about whether their toys are getting to move too. They may need some time with all of their things before you can slowly remove the things they no longer use.

If you are the only one around, or choose to not have your child present, set aside a box of the things that you know they have grown out of or have gotten too old for. Put the box away before your child gets a chance to see what you have taken. Hold onto it for a few months. If your child doesn't even realize what is missing and never asks where it went, then you should be safe to remove it from your house. This is a VERY effective method in de-cluttering any child's room, even when relocation is not a factor.

<u>Notes</u>

A Place for Everything

Hopefully, you are not opening this chapter too long after reviewing the tasks in the 'Delivery Day'. By now you should have found a place for most things. Perhaps you are still unpacking and finding it difficult to divide it all into the three groups. **Keep**, **Sell/Donate** and **Discard**, we established in the previous chapter. If so, let me give you a little perspective. Think back to how simply you were living during your time of transition. You did just fine with the few things you had packed in your suitcase. You have dealt with the minimum of luxuries. It is understood that each new home you live in and each moving experience can be over-whelming. It is a constant and challenging task to settle in, knowing you will eventually be moving out. Trying to find the best place for every household item can be a difficult, time consuming and a huge project. In this chapter, let's open your mind to the world of ORGANIZATION. If you consider yourself an unorganized person, there are basic organizaing concepts that can turn you around.

When you begin putting the '**Keep**' items away, don't just shove them in where they fit. Evaluate each item and think about where it belongs best. How often it is used can determine how far back it goes, or on which shelf it sits.

Decide where in the house are you most likely to use it, and put it there. For example, if you do your gift-wrapping in the kitchen, then those items should be stored there, not in the closet in the attic. If the attic is the only place they fit, then section off a space or "zone" in the attic and have a small side table designated for gift-wrapping with a box close by that holds paper, scissors, tape, tags and ribbons. The need to hunt for it all each time you need it is eliminated. This method can be used in the office, kitchen, etc.

Creating correct zones, from the beginning, will allow the normal routine of household duties to fall into place with minimal effort. Along with this simple organizational skill will come the beneficial time and money-saving techniques you need so desperately. It will be time saving by knowing what you have and where it is; no more rummaging through closets and basements. It will be money saving by preventing you from an impulse shopping trip to buy what you can't find as well as picking up more unnecessary junk since you are out anyway. The funny thing about that is, usually within the day you get back from shopping, you find the exact thing you were looking for in the first place. Being more organized, shopping trips like these could be avoided and you will save money and resist buying more things to fill up your already cluttered space. So think twice as you are filling your cabinets and closets. In the long run it is worth taking the time initially to get a little organized than waiting until it is too late and too overwhelming.

If you followed the advice in Delivery Day, regarding the '**3-box-method**' of organizing, the ideas and steps to organization will require much less effort. If you found it hard to sort as you were unpacking, or got to this chapter a little late and have already stuffed it all away, set aside this organizing time and allow yourself another opportunity to do so. Many times you will find yourself realizing that even though you have already sorted and de-cluttered, you still seem to find more things that you just don't use. It is somewhat addicting once you get into the habit. You begin to look for things you don't use or need. Your space becomes more controllable. Your favorite items now can are noticed, no longer hiding behind disorder.

Organizing is a constant household task. Once you begin to understand its simplicity, you will find every thing in life finds order as well, not just in your home, but your household schedule, your personal free time, your clothing wardrobe and your daily responsibilities. Clutter and stress go hand-in-hand. Do you ever find yourself trying to relax by watching television or reading a book, but you just can't seem to stay focused because you know that there are more important things that need to be done, such as cleaning out the filing cabinet or sorting through your photos? This causes stress. If there is order in the things around us, it is easier to give ourselves the quality personal attention we all need. Try it, you'll feel it working.

A common habit among the disorganized is keeping old things that have long since been replaced. If you bought a new blender because the old one just wouldn't blend, then why is there a need to keep it? It belongs in the '**Discard**' box. Don't try to sell it or even give it away. If it isn't working for you, it will not work for someone else. Merchandise like appliances, computer parts and other electronics are not built to last a lifetime. They are built to last a few years or until a new style is introduced, which seems to happen at the exact moment your current one breaks. Isn't it funny how that industry works? So don't feel bad or be afraid to throw the old one away.

Another area in a home that tends to become over-whelming is our closets. The linen closet especially, is meant to include, bed sheets, bath towels, dishtowels, tablecloths, blankets, curtains and off-season clothing. This area is mentioned because it tends to be a problem area for most. It is always a surprise to open "linen" closets and find batteries, extension cords, unfinished children's craft projects and even a re-gift box. Since closet space is normally limited in  government quarters or non-existent in some European homes, it is alright to use closet spaces for multiple functions. However, there is a difference between keeping spaces full and keeping spaces organized. Let there be a limit to the amount of things you close behind closet doors and these little hidden nooks can almost become another functional room.

So your multi-functional closet could look something like this…the top shelf has labeled clear bins that hold Batteries, Light bulbs and Extension Cords, Sewing supplies and a hot glue gun. The second shelf holds bins labeled for children's craft supplies (Beads, Paints, Stickers, etc.). The third shelf is a gift-wrapping station with a bin of "re-gifts" and a basket with scissors, ribbon and tags. Also here are tissue paper and gift bags. The last shelf can be for household linens, guest pillows and tablecloths. This is an example of using a single purpose space for a multi-purpose function. Ideas like this come about by being, as mentioned earlier, open-minded.

Trends and transformations in home interior styles are continually changing. Just when you've completed the brown and pink bathroom of your dreams, orange hits the scene as the "in" color. If you are like many, and love the "in" things, then you will know what this industry is all about. Be very selective when choosing, for instance, new linens. Quality linens can be very expensive and color and pattern trends change almost monthly. If you enjoy the feel of fine linens like Egyptian cotton and 600 thread count sheets, be sure to stick with the tried and true neutral color scheme. The focus in this chapter is not color; however, it needs to be mentioned briefly when choosing these high priced point commodities. You can never go wrong with white and beige. Stay neutral and classic when you are in the market for high quality.

If you are worried about keeping up with the trends, don't be. There are a variety of options to choose from to enhance your home décor. Accent pieces are the

best way to keep your home looking fresh and trendy. Accent pieces can range from collectibles to artwork, from paint to pillows. No need for pricey pieces. There are many stores that carry 'knock-offs' or originals at a deep discount. Also check out your local flea markets, outlets and second hand stores. By purchasing accent items from these types of shops, it is more affordable to keep up with what is current and change things frequently without a huge investment. Go back to the instance regarding the pink and brown bathroom. If the towels, rugs and main accessories are in the white and beige family, then a vase and maybe a hand towel or two can be the focal point of the color trend. This holds true in most rooms in your house.

Look around. What are the focal points in each room? Is it a bowl? A chair? A blanket? Pick out an item, make it the focus of the room, and reduce the amount of clutter you have around it. It will get noticed and you will appear to have your decorating act together.

Collecting dishes is a very easy habit to develop. You may have an everyday set, a formal set (maybe not even complete since most was probably a wedding gift), the hand-me-down set or college set. I bet most of you even have plastic or melamine sets (for the kids) and picnic sets. Besides taking up a lot of space in the kitchen cabinets, they are taking up space in basements, closets and other storage style pieces of furniture throughout your house. Dishes are very heavy and make a huge impact on your weight allowance when you move. The space they take up is also very valuable to you. Remember about creating spaces for a purpose? Who uses dishes in the basement? Narrow down to your favorites and most used sets. Donate the others to your installation loan closet or other organization. Let the kids help in picking their favorites and donating the rest. Think of all the additional space you will have for

other things. If you must keep dishes in storage, there are a number of good storage options available designed for that purpose. Perfectly sized, soft or hard-sided bins can safely hold your treasured collections.

Like dishes, books can accumulate very rapidly and manage to find their way into every room. Likewise, they are heavy. Most of the books in your house were purchased, read once and then put on the shelf…just in case you want to read

it again. Rarely do these book get touched more than that once, except to be packed up for a move again. The easiest way to realize how many books you have and downsize your library is to put the entire book collection in one place. When I refer to a collection, I mean novels, textbooks, magazines, reference materials, cookbooks and children's books.

Divide the books into categories. Evaluate each category of books and pick out the ones you use on a monthly basis. Yes, monthly! Those books are the ones to go back on the shelf first. If you do not have a bookshelf or shelving unit you may have something else that can accommodate your new library. Wait until you are finished purging to determine the proper size your storage

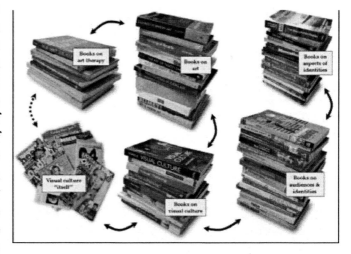

should be. If certain books belong to other members in the family, give them an appropriate size box in which to place the books they want to keep.

Donate any gently used books to the public library, local schools or community businesses such as a doctor's office. Once you have established your **Keep** pile you can make a storage purchase to fit your needs. How about a hope chest, trunk or small cabinet? Think of alternative uses for something you already own. For books like cookbooks or reference materials, return them to their room-specific spaces. If you use the cookbooks in your kitchen, it is best you store them there.

When returning books to their shelves, there is a proper way to arrange them. Because they are in view all the time, you want to be sure they become part of the design of the room. Keep the paperbacks on separate shelves from the hard covers. The hardcover books should go on the shelves closest to the center of the unit. By pulling each book forward, flush to the edge of the shelf, you create an even, more modern appearance. Patterning the books and keeping each shelf different from the other breaks up the monotony, and the focus of the unit becomes a work of art.

If your bookcase is tall, the hard-covered books will be at eye-level. If you have a bookcase that is more of a credenza style that is short and wide, the heavier hardcover books should be on the bottom shelf keeping a lower balance to the bookcase. Leaving the smaller paperbacks on the top shelves and adding interesting artifacts to the horizontal stacks is very artistic and good design practice. Separate the books on the shelves by size, standing the shorter books on their ends and lay larger books that will not fit vertically.

The best accessories for the library are items pertaining to the hobby of reading (glasses, magnifying glass or a small candle lamp) or

items that are the subject matters of the books themselves (travel souvenirs, statues or life memorabilia). Keep same-sized books together for cleaner lines and a finished look.

For the avid book collector whose library is rather extensive, the same standards should apply. Keeping them categorized by author, genre or alphabetical will help them to be found easier when they are desired. Be sure to stand some vertically and lay others down once in a while. A shelf that is lined with books can be obtrusive to a room's décor. If the shelving used is deep, paperback books can be stored behind the hard covers to maximize the shelf space. Keep similar sorts on the same level.

Periodicals and catalogs often have articles, websites or photos of things you wish to keep for future reading, project ideas or things you may want to purchase. Because we like to hold on to these valuable references, most people will stash them away in a basket or closet, never managing to get them out and use them for the reason they kept them. This common habit takes up space and is one that needs to be broken!

If you are a collector of certain periodicals and save every issue, invest in proper magazine storage or sturdy boxes.

Labeling the file boxes by date or issue number will keep the magazines easily accessible and look nice sitting on a shelf where they are in view.

If saving the complete magazine is not what you had in mind, the best way to keep these ideas handy, without having to keep all the advertisements and useless pages that are attached to it, is to create a file system for only the pages you wish to save. Purchase an accordion file folder or three-ring binder and a few page dividers.

Label the dividers into categories such as Home Projects, Web Resources, Articles of Interest, Gift Ideas and Future Purchases. Tear or cut from the magazines and catalogs the pages of interest to you.

Using the binder or an accordion pocket folder to categorize your articles will make them easier to find when you need them. It also cuts down on the amount of space taken up by all the editions of magazines. When you receive a new catalog in the mail, save the page you want from the previous mailing and then discard it. Keeping handy only current issues in the basket or pile will not only look better, but will save a lot of space. Retail catalogs change out less than 5% of their product inventory between printings. If there is one idea you just have to save, into the binder it goes. Keep in mind that

most periodicals and store catalogs are easily accessible via the World Wide Web. By logging on to their website, you can download the exact page you need and save it to a file on your computer. No space wasted here at all.

There are circumstances that arise, when moving, that are never easy to avoid. The biggest of these is storage. Not your clothes closets and hall closets, the storage we're talking about here are the extra areas in the home, apart from the rooms in which we live in. There never seems to be enough of it. Whether it is a closet, basement, garage or attic, storage space poses a problem when it comes to organizing your home.

Many homes in government housing provide you with a small closet intended to hold your holiday decorations, off season items, hobby supplies and household goods you do not use everyday. Government housing in Europe and other locations provide you with a variety of storage areas. Stairwell apartments usually have a cage or locked cubby space in the basement or attic. A utility shed located outdoors can be another type. There are solutions to every storage dilemma, and we are going to tackle them one at a time.

No matter what type of storage you have or how much space you have to work with, you will initially have to make a good attempt to clean out your storage inventory.

- Get rid of the things you have been lugging around through every PCS, always thinking you will use it, but never do.
- Make repairs to what needs fixing, so it can be a useful item instead of a space taker. If you can't fix it, you don't need it.
- Throw away paint cans that contain paint colors from a house you no longer live in. Small portions that are still needed for touch-ups can be downsized into smaller utility cans, glass jars (recycled food jars) or plastic Tupperware® containers. If they have been sitting in a can too long, check their consistency and throw away if they are too thick or lumpy.
- Sort through old clothes and children's items that you have been hanging on to. If they don't fit, you don't need them.
- Categorize your belongings. This will help determine the type of storage solution you need.
- Evaluate your sports equipment, camping gear, car accessories, holiday items, old electronics, papers and textbooks, luggage, tools and furniture. It you have replaced any old with something new, it is time to move on and leave the past behind.

Once that task is complete you will have a much clearer understanding of what you need to store and how you are going to store it.

Government quarters may have a storage shed outside in the yard or on the side of the house. It is not too common to move into housing, especially older construction, and find yourself without a basement or a garage. This limited storage space makes it difficult for military families to find order in their home when everything they own has to be in view. The architects and builders of newer housing communities have taken this storage issue into consideration and are, in many cases, increasing the amount of storage space.

When space inside your home is minimal and you are searching for another

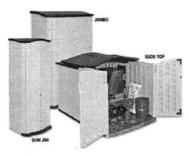

storage option, turn to Rubbermaid®. They have developed a complete line of outdoor storage units that will serve your smallest or largest storage needs. The features that make these units favorable to moving families are that they can be assembled and disassembled without the use of any tools and are composed of a nominal amount of pieces. Made of plastic, they withstand all weather conditions and are water resistant. Available in many sizes, they can hold sports equipment, holiday decorations, toys, etc. Not only ideal for use outdoors, but also in garages and basements. In the circumstances where you must share a storage area with other families, these sheds come with an option for a padlock to be inserted.

Alternative metal or PVC shelving systems are available and come in many sizes as well. They can be bought in pieces that can custom fit into the tiniest and largest of storage spaces. It

is easier to use items from storage if they are easily accessible and not buried under other things. Shelving systems can either be installed permanently or they can be disassembled and taken to your next assignment. If you are going to be putting your house on the market before you move, built-in storage systems are a wise investment and a big bonus for a buyer, especially if you are selling in a military community.

Private rental homes or homes that have been purchased usually have one major form of storage or another. If you have this additional storage space in your home, treat a garage, a basement and an attic as three separate storage areas that are meant to serve you three separate purposes. They will be three new custom spaces to keep your possessions organized.

Use the following lists to prioritize your needs and create a space that will accommodate your storage items, and use them as a guide as to what belongs where. Following the storage **Keep**, **Sell/ Donate** or **Discard** lists, easily identified by the icons presented in 'Delivery Day'.

Keep   **Sell/Donate**   **Discard**

Attic

- Family heirlooms/ photos
- Small Furniture/ Antiques
- Out-of-season clothing
- Holiday decorations

A drop down ladder, located in a hallway ceiling, usually accesses the attic storage space. The entrance into the attic can be small and get rather tight if you and a piece of furniture try to fit up at the same time. It is typically an unfinished space (no walls, just insulation) that is dry and warm. The attic is the perfect environment for items that need to be away from moisture. Be aware of the ventilation system, fiberglass insulation and any electrical wires. The attic is ideal for storing items that need to be temperature controlled. The attic is a potential location for fires to start. Therefore, be sure to install a smoke/fire alarm if one does not exist.

Most heirloom items such as photo albums and memorabilia should be kept away from humid and damp environments. Moisture can create an ideal situation for molds to grow, which would certainly ruin anything. Because most government housing or rental properties do not have or do not allow access to the attic, heirloom items should be kept in sealed containers.

Photos should be stored in acid free and lignin-free paper, boxes or albums.

This storage will prevent photos from becoming brittle and yellowed. It is advisable to have your heirloom photos professionally copied and stored onto cd-roms. Provide a family member with a set of these photos. It is smart to have a back-up if your household goods get damaged. Photo albums that contain static adhesive pages are not advisable for photo storage. These pages contain an acid that will discolor your photographs over time and when their adhesive dries, the photos will be impossible to remove without additional harm. Because of their delicate nature, photos should be stored in an area that does not get too hot either. Heat will dry them out causing them to become brittle and they may crack. If your space allows, you may consider storing your photos in a bedroom, closet or cabinet. The temperature and air quality within the living area of your home is much more conducive to their preservation.

An attic is also a good place to store your out-of-season clothing. Clothes are best kept on hangers on a rod or in boxes. Sweaters should be kept off the hangers to prevent sagging and stretching, folded in a box is best. It is important to remove the plastic bags used by dry cleaners from any

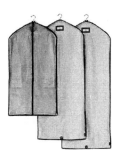

stored clothing. The plastic contain chemicals that can discolor your textiles.

The solvent used in the dry cleaning process also contains high levels of chemicals. If you prefer to store your occasional clothing under wraps, do so in properly designed garment bags. Free standing closet systems are the perfect solution to housing your formal attire, military uniforms and out-of-season accessories. Keeping your garments aired and well ventilated is the best way to store them.

✳— Make your own garment bags. Cut a small notch in the closed end of a pillowcase. Slide the clothing, on the hanger, into the pillowcase and feed the hanger through the notch you cut.

Basement

- Holiday decorations (in plastic bins)
- Out-of-season sport equipment/ Outdoor toys/ Patio furniture
- Household repair items (paint, furniture, etc)
- Out-of-season clothing (in plastic bins)
- Fans/ air conditioners

An unfinished basement or crawl space is typically a damp or moist storage area. Items stored here should be those that can withstand cooler temperatures. If needed, the use of plastic storage containers or a dehumidifier can be very beneficial

when storing more environmentally sensitive items. If your basement is prone to flooding, raise your storage items off the floor with wood pallets or wood boards (2"x4"). Keep a path clear to your fuse box and Main power switches. Also keep the areas around water heaters and electrical wires clear.

The best plastic storage containers in the market are made by Rubbermaid®. They come in various colors, shapes and sizes and can suit all your storage needs. They stack nicely on top of each other and can withstand even the toughest of moves. They even come in clear so you can see the contents of your storage.

The basement is the biggest catchall space around. You may find yourself regularly carrying things to the basement. You take down things for the next yard sale, things to put into storage, fans, extra pantry items, and the list goes on. But the difference between being organized and not, is actually having a yard sale, putting things into their properly label storage containers, eating the pantry items you buy, and using the sports equipment you have purchased.

Garage

- Tools
- Car cleaners, supplies (buckets, hoses, sponges)
- Lawn and garden items
- Bicycles or motorcycle and helmets
- Children's outdoor toys (skates, jump ropes, balls)

The garage, Wow! Have you ever driven down the street and taken a good look into garages. It is amazing what people store in there. Usually there is only room for one car if any at all. The garage was designed originally for your car, and things you need for your car. It was to prevent your car from being damaged by

environmental situations, such as hail, falling leaves and sap from trees. It was meant to provide you with a dry place to load or unload your family in a rainstorm, or unload groceries. Often being the only storage space in government housing, it must fulfill alternative duties, not only housing a vehicle but also a number of other things. Today for many, however, the garage has become just another place to put more 'stuff' you are not using. Again, there are various storage systems designed for those garage storage needs.

Now, it is understood that you may or may not have all of these storage conveniences in your government quarters, rental property or your owned home. The important thing to consider before storing something is whether or not you will eventually get it out and use it. If you find yourself hauling around the same boxes or belongings, move after move, and storing them away each time, these are most likely things you don't use. They would make better use to you if they were out of your house, donated or sold and replaced with a few extra dollar bills. Better use because you would then have additional areas to use for something else, a space you can create for a specific need. When you have narrowed down what you are going to store, you can decide the best place and way to store it.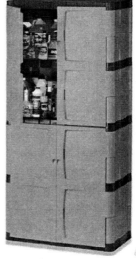

As transient people and families, living in a variety of different styles of housing, it is impossible to specify exactly how much to keep and how much to let go of each and every time you move.

The following is a **'3-box-method'** list to help you begin your storage organization project:

✓ Sports Equipment in good working condition ✓ Family heirlooms and memorabilia ✓ Holiday decorations that you enjoy and display ✓ Tools in good condition ✓ Non-perishable pantry items ✓ Extra furniture and household goods ✓ Off-season clothing ✓ Automotive supplies for current vehicles ✓ Gardening tools and decorations ✓ Luggage that is operational ✓ Extra linens and bedding	✓ Electronics and appliances that work well ✓ Furniture you have grown out of ✓ Sports equipment too small for family members ✓ Baby equipment and clothing ✓ Duplicate tools and hardware items ✓ Books and reference material gently used ✓ VHS tapes and music cassettes you now longer view or listen to ✓ Dishes and kitchen items in incomplete sets ✓ Exercise equipment you no longer use	✓ Rusty and broken tools and hardware ✓ Worn out and moth-eaten clothing ✓ Old paint from prior homes ✓ Stained baby items ✓ Toys that are missing pieces ✓ Outdated computer parts ✓ Broken garden pots and flower boxes ✓ Expired pantry items ✓ Broken furniture and household accessories ✓ VHS tapes with recorded television shows ✓ Broken dishes and glasses

Here is an example. Your current house has two and a half bathrooms. That means, at the minimum, you own probably three different color schemes of towels and accessories. Now you move, and the next house has only one full bathroom. Does that mean you pick your favorites or what matches the sink and chuck the rest? Only to move yet again, back to two full bathrooms. Certainly not! One goal of 'That Military House' is to help you make smart choices when it comes to decorating and organizing your home.

Recall earlier I mentioned to keep towels and the like to neutral colors. This is helpful in this situation. All the towels, etc. will match all the possibilities in all of your living conditions. If there are a few accents or off-colored items from previous rooms, they can be placed in one appropriately sized plastic bin, stored very minimally, clearly labeled as 'Bathroom Accessories'. Attempting to store bulky items such as towels and rugs can really consume space.

The ever-so-popular storage technique of using bins and labels didn't get its reputation by accident. This system is multi-functional and so simple that it can be useful throughout the entire house. When purchasing bins, be sure to stick with one brand. They should stack very neatly if they have similar dimensions. As mentioned earlier, Rubbermaid® is highly recommended because they not only keep things dry, but they are virtually indestructible. They are flexible enough to fill, and rugged enough to support many moves. Do not get caught up in choosing brands that draw you in with fun colors and shapes. Although tempting, these bins are for your storage, tucked away where only you will see them.  Decorative containers also have a much higher price point. Save your money when buying storage bins for the basement, attic and garage. You can add a bit of interest and variety by choosing colors that represent what you are keeping inside. How about red for Christmas and white for extra linens and so forth? Choosing colors can also help you spot different storage items easily. Storage specific bins are designed to hold task specific supplies, such as gift wrap, holiday wreaths and sports equipment, to name a few.

If the bins will be in a room where they are part of your decorating and organizing solution, then choose ones that are a little more appealing and serve a purpose at the same time. Buy enough for your present storage needs and then some, all at the same time, while store supplies last. You will most likely enjoy and appreciate the way they look and want a few more.

Usually things that are trendy don't stay on the store shelves very long. They sell quickly and are minimally stocked. Your retailers know and understand the home interior industry and they don't want to be stuck with last month's hot items, only to timely be replaced with the "new" thing.

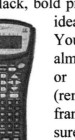

Labeling your storage containers makes it easy to find what you are looking for without opening each one to look inside. Clear containers are great because you can see through them, but if they are large and are full to the rim, you'll only see a portion of the items you are storing inside. Clear bins are good for smaller quantity items that are kept in closets and pantries. Labels with black, bold printed letters on a white background are ideal, easy for everyone to read and to see. You can buy an inexpensive label maker almost anywhere, from your AAFES, NEX or similar military installation store (remember: no sales tax there) to a franchised home office supply store. Be sure to stock up on additional cartridges, you'll eventually get label happy and run out midway through an organizing project.

Here is a bit of advice and a cost-effective tip. When you begin using a label maker; get the most out of the label cartridge by filling the typing area until the memory is full. Leave only one space between words and then cut between the spaces with scissors later. Avoid the fancy borders and cool self-cutting tool. Each time you print and cut using the machine's cutting tool, there is a lot of wasted label space on either side of the word or words. Minimize that, and your cartridge will go much further. If you only need one label for the moment, write the word or words on a Post-it® note and stick it to the label maker.

When you have accumulated several words, print them out at the same time. In the meantime, use another Post-it® to label your container until the labels are printed. Remember, however, if you change the contents of the box, change the label too.

Hopefully, by now, you are inspired to make some big and necessary organizational changes and advancements to your way of life. So, get to those storage areas and have a good try. Make the best effort you can! At first, the job will be huge, but as time passes, you'll feel better, your house will look better and you will be prepared for easier and more efficient moves.

<u>Notes</u>

<u>Notes</u>

Color:
It's what holds it all together

Now that you are settled in, and your new house is beginning to function normally, it is time to get creative and add some personal touches to your new surroundings. Maybe you would like some new curtains, different color paint on the walls or even a new look all together. You have seen numerous home makeover shows on television and maybe have an idea and plan already in mind. But how do you do it all? Where do you start?

Let's start with choosing or focusing on one room and its color scheme. Assuming you have already de-cluttered and re-organized what you could in that room, you can now pick out what your featured item will be. Is it an armchair given to you by your family? Possibly, it is a piece of art that you have acquired on a vacation. This item may be composed of many colors. Look closely at the little details. Find all the colors that are in the fabric or paint materials. Does one of the minor or less obvious colors strike you as one you would like to develop a room around? Your focal point in the room will look best and become enhanced by choosing a color that is not the brightest or most concentrated among them all. A color that is subtle and involved minimally in a pattern will be the best for that room.

Next, think about the purpose of the room. Is it a getaway for relaxation, work and sleep? Maybe it is a family area or a room used mostly for entertainment. There are literally millions of color choices available, but you can easily narrow down the choices by knowing the purpose of the room or the mood you would like to create for those who spend time there. Each color possesses special characteristics, and naturally creates feelings when we surround ourselves within them.

If you are having difficulty deciding on a color, you can take a look at a color wheel. Most professional decorators and designers use this tool to determine which colors go best together to compliment items of and achieve the desires of their clients. A color wheel is very simple to use and only has a few steps and rules to follow. If you are sticking with an existing wall color or furniture color scheme, that's okay. You can still use the wheel to make decisions about what to add to your existing pieces to create the mood you want. Hirshfield's has one of the best visual aids on-line at www.hirshfields.com.

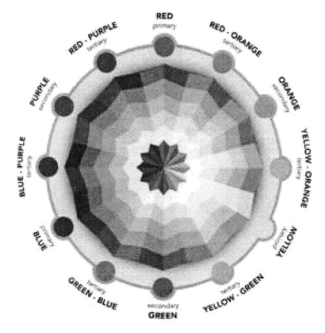

The colors red, orange and yellow are 'warm colors'. Opposite them are blue, green and purple. These are the 'cool colors'. The colors next to each other determine how warm or how cool each color can be. There are three major color combinations that will develop from the choices you make. They are Monochromatic, Analogous and Complementary.

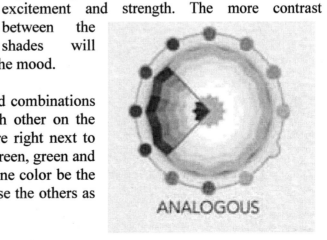

Warm and Cool Palettes

Monochromatic combinations consist of one color or hue of that color that just varies in intensity of each other. For example, three different values of red. These combinations create the mood that is directly related to the color. For red, the mood created is full of high emotions. It represents depth and passion. It stimulates our senses to feel excitement and strength. The more contrast

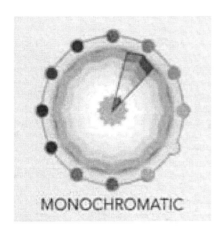

MONOCHROMATIC

between the shades will create a more dramatic affect of the mood.

The Analogous or Related combinations use colors that are close to each other on the color wheel, those colors that are right next to one another. For example: blue-green, green and yellow-green. In this choice let one color be the dominant or primary color and use the others as accents or secondary colors.

ANALOGOUS

The Complementary or Contrasting combinations use the colors that are opposites on the color wheel. Red and green, blue and orange and purple and yellow. Although these color combinations may seem drastic, when put in a room within closeness of each other, they make the mood of the room exciting and will tend to draw in your attention. This happens very often in nature and most people don't even realize it; purple flowers with yellow centers, a red rose with green leaves. If you lighten or darken each of the colors, the room remains calm yet at the same time will keep the visual excitement.

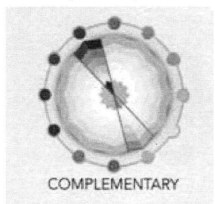

COMPLEMENTARY

When you are deciding on a color scheme for a room, and you want to have three predominant colors, you can choose colors that are considered to be Split Complimentary. Your most represented color would be isolated and the other two colors would be less of a focus.

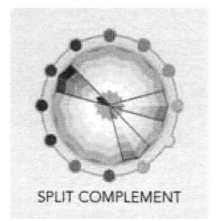

SPLIT COMPLEMENT

If you decide you would like to have all three of your color choices used equally throughout the design, you would look at the color wheel and make your selections based on the Triadic theory. This would allow you to create a balance in the room, without one color overpowering any other.

TRIADIC

With an understanding of what you have just learned, look at the descriptions for the basic colors and see where it takes you. First, let's learn about the warm palette.

Red - Red is a color that is full of high emotions. It represents depth and passion. It stimulates our senses to feel excitement and strength. In every culture, red is the strongest color. It is the highest color in the rainbow; it is the beginning of the color spectrum and has the longest wavelength. It instantly commands our attention, used in banners and in our flag. It's believed to be one of the first colors a baby sees.

Red brings with it the message of achievement and glory shown in some cultures by blood and fire. It has been associated with a life force from the beginning of our existence. In its fiery tones it can be majestic and passionate. Those of high honor are given the red carpet treatment for a purpose. It can also be very intense and powerful; teachers use red ink to correct papers, when we are in debt financially we consider ourselves to be "in the red".

The excitement we feel when we encounter the color red is more physiological than we realize. When we see the color red, our body naturally releases adrenalin, it creates more frequent eye blinking and an increase in blood pressure, respiration and heartbeat. Our senses are affected by red. Adrenaline can also cause our sense of smell to be heightened, our appetite to increase and our taste buds to become more sensitive to the foods we eat. That's why most people prefer the red pieces of candy or the red colored Popsicle. Studies show that our brain shows the most activity when we see red. Notice the next time you are out on the town, look at all the red lights!

Variations of Red: Crimson, Cardinal, Scarlet, Cherry, Poppy, Cranberry, Maroon, Garnet and Burgundy

Pink - Pink is noted for creating the feeling of youthfulness. It is playful and energetic and joyful. It represents things soft and innocent. Pink is a version of red with much of the same emotions and passion, so it creates a feeling of happiness rather than excitement. When things are going well in life we "see the world through rose-colored glasses". When we get a touch of sun and our cheekbones get pink, we look healthy and vibrant. Pink is sexy with a bit of innocence. In their hotter forms, pink can have the same statement as red.

In different cultures pink has many meanings. Lighter, softer pinks are favorites in castles and great halls. When painted in rooms, it can make the room feel airy and spirited. It has been the favorite color for the ladies of the harem; imagine soft pink ladies, dancing and casting their silhouette shadows against the white marble halls of the elite. Pink is often accented by shades of green (note they are complementary).

The fashion industry has captured pink throughout the years. It seems to find its place in every trend. Magenta was developed in 1859 as one of the first synthetic dyes. It became very popular for the Victorians who loved the hues in velvet, damasks and taffetas, all exquisite textiles that hold a high value. By the 1920s, the use of make-up was acceptable and pink was the preferred and favorite color for the cheeks, with red on the lips. In the 1940s, it hit the interior decorating scene.

Lately being paired with shades of brown, it has yet again been voted one of the most popular colors schemes of all time.

Variations of Pink: Wild Rose, Ash, Azalea, Powder, Candy, Strawberry, Hot Pink, and Fuchsia

Orange - Orange can create a feeling of warmth. It lifts our spirits and makes us feel happy and joyous. Its varying shades make up the color of the sunset. It is the link between red and yellow. There is no cool tone to orange. Everything about it is luminous and hot because it takes its heat from two very exciting neighboring colors.

In history, the color orange, as well as its same name fruit, has been used to symbolize love. Giving and receiving oranges were a traditional way to make someone feel appreciated. The orange scent is considered to be an aphrodisiac and in Greece it symbolized adultery. In the Middle Ages, orange's love connection eventually took a turn for the worse and became known for false love and deceit.

Of all the colors in the spectrum, orange is the least understood. It can seem to bold or too noisy. The deeper shades of orange, adding a brown tone, have become popular. Terracotta and coral for instance are shades that are typically more desirable to ones taste. Orange is quickly associated to time of harvest or Halloween. Many people think it is too representative of

a pumpkin and rarely find anything to match that suits their room décor. It is also used a lot in advertising to grab the attention of the customer.

Variations of Orange: Cantaloupe, Apricot, Papaya, Melon, Coral, Terracotta and Summer Squash

Yellow - Yellow stands for and is noted for energy, happiness and a joyful life. It reflects the sun and all feelings the sun brings with it. It is radiant and bright, and warms a room with even the most minimal of shades. Yellow signifies an example of intelligence. In most cultures, yellow and gold express status and prestige. Gold is the finest of all precious metals. Yellow dyes were made from saffron, the most expensive of spices. Others who could not afford such luxuries made their yellow dyes from buckwheat and safflower blossoms, attempting to achieve the same beautiful range of color.

Yellow is very important to the color wheel because it is needed to make the secondary colors of green and orange. It is illuminating and reflects light very well. It is used in signs of caution and rarely goes unnoticed. Studies show that yellow is most often associated with words like cheerful, joyful, and sunny. Like the reds, it increases heart rate and respiration and alleviates depression.

When in doubt you can always choose a shade of yellow to compliment any style of furniture or room functionality. A light shade of yellow, like butter, is the new white and can make a positive and welcoming change to dull environments.

Varieties of Yellow: Lemonade, Dandelion, Primrose, Nugget, Canary and Popcorn

The cool colors have similar and just as emotional histories and backgrounds.

Blue - Blue is symbolic of the sea and sky. It is a color of cleanliness and freshness. It is peaceful and relaxing. It is the color of constancy and truth. Blue is special in the

fact that it goes with every color. It can be found in every part of nature, especially the sky, and is used, because of its primary nature, to create an abundance of other colors for us in the spectrum. There is a sense of peace when we look at blue for any given time. It is regarded universally as the color of the spirit.

Blue, in many cultures, is used as protection against the forces of evil. In the southwest, many Native Americans paint their front doors blue

for this purpose. In Greece, a piece of blue cloth is pinned to a baby's undergarments to ward off bad spirits. Many years ago, Indigo was used to dye fabrics blue, in combination with other earth elements like fruit and ash. Blue has been used to signify victory over battles, immortality and supremacy.

Physiologically, looking at blue lowers blood pressure, heartbeat and respiration. It is an excellent color for ceilings in small spaces, creating a height and openness.

Variations of Blue: Dresden, China, Wedgwood, Chalk, Celestial and Powder, Cobalt, Midnight and Navy

Green - Green signifies newness and birth. It is life-giving. It is the color of nature and surrounds us with healing emotions. It is a very restful color for the eye. The natural responses for green run from richness and praise, to disgust and grossness. There are almost 10 million variations on green that are discernable to the human eye. Green is believed to be the first color to appear on the Earth and very important for survival. Most edible plants in the beginning of time were some form of green, and still are today.

Green is abundant in nature and can be located in the forms of plants, which are fruitful and nurturing, but can also be noticed in the insects' colonies and creatures that exist in this world too.

Green can lead our thoughts to eternal peacefulness and rest. It is a very soothing color. The softer shades of green are very popular for wellness centers and health spas due to their restful qualities. What better reason for Mother Nature to use green as the main color in her palate. Our sense of smell is brought stronger to things with the shade of green, like limes and cut grass. It is the perfect color to put with all others. It matches almost everything.

The word 'green' comes from the same root as 'grow,' so green symbolizes that which grows as well as the regeneration and renewal of life. In many religions green carries implications of immortality, faith and contemplation. Blue-Greens are associated with the sea, which is calm, spacious and cool. Aqua is actually a word of romantic language, meaning "water", or "sea". The origin of the word 'turquoise' comes from the French meaning 'Turkish' because the stone was first brought from Turkey to France. Teal green is seen as sophisticated and upscale.

Variations of Green: Olive, Jade, Sage and Eucalyptus

Purple - Purple is the color of wealth and luxury. It signifies dignity and romance. Purple is the color of authority. Purple is the most energetic of all colors. It is a

combination of Red and Blue. It is the most complex color in the rainbow, from passionate red-violets to strong, silent indigos. Chromo-therapists, those who study the effects of color on individuals, claim that purple light has the power to heal conditions like hacking coughs, hoarseness, high blood pressure, and even lunacy. The oils of violets were used for medicinal purposes in medieval times mostly for insomnia.

The most precious dye color in the ancient world was purple. The Phoenicians discovered the purple hue in a shellfish, purpuridae. Only a single drop of mucous could be extracted from each tiny mollusk. That made the dye very expensive because you needed a lot to get the rich hues of pigment. Approximately 336,000 snails were needed to produce one ounce of dye! There is a certain mystical or spiritual quality attached to purple. Violet has the highest frequency in the visible spectrum and many mystics and New Age believers see violet as the highest spiritual intuition.

In religion, specifically referenced in the Old Testament, purple is associated with splendor and dignity. It also holds symbolic memories of suffering and sacrifice. Some writers and historians believe that the original 'purple' was possibly magenta or crimson. When dyed onto wool, in robes, it took on a plum color. In Egypt, amethyst was cherished as a healing amulet, a protection from evil. Wearing an amethyst was thought to bring peace of mind and encourage positive dreaming.

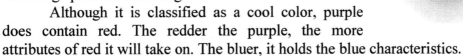

Although it is classified as a cool color, purple does contain red. The redder the purple, the more attributes of red it will take on. The bluer, it holds the blue characteristics.

Variations of Purple: Lilac, Orchid, Mauve, Lavender, Pansy, Eggplant and Violet

Black - Black is a very formal color. Believe it or not, black is a color of faithfulness. It is naturally calming and promotes order and it is sleek and sophisticated. Yet, black to some is sinister and eerie. In fact, no other color evokes such a wide variety of emotions. It goes from magical and mysterious to foreboding and funeral-like, suave and sexy to dark and sober. No matter how it appears, one thing remains true, it is always noticed. One small accent of black in a room can change the look completely. Black is one of the first colors that we associate to as infants. Black had come to denote chic-ness as well as the ultimate in elegance and drama. It also signifies solid, basic strength.

Decorating with black has its place. It would be too much to cover your walls in black, but a floor or many accent  pieces would be eye-catching. Black adds elegance to any room perhaps in a sofa or lampshade or one focal piece of furniture. Black also makes an imposing trim color on the exterior of a house. Black shutters on a white or pale color house signify that someone powerful resides in that home.

Every room should contain one object that is black. This decorating technique allows our eye to see the other colors as they are, black giving the eye a reference point.

The timeless combination of black and white will forever be acceptable. They are in fact symbolic of the ancient Chinese dualistic philosophy of the yin and yang forces. In your home, however, a third color should be introduced to balance the contrast and allow a smooth transition and a comfortable environment.

Brown - Brown is a secure color. It is the neutral that blends all colors together. It signifies nature and gives a sense of safety. Brown is the color of the earth and of being home, of dried herbs and stone-ground grains. It represents strength, like the oak tree and stability like the roots.

Brown is easily attainable with little or no cost as a dye from natural sources. It represents those who are humble and hard-working. Although brown in wood tones is not often thought of as a color, it still has a psychological presence. Even those who express a dislike in the color brown will often surround themselves with brown wood furnishings and hard wood floors.

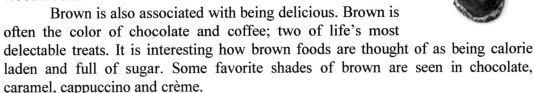

Brown is also associated with being delicious. Brown is often the color of chocolate and coffee; two of life's most delectable treats. It is interesting how brown foods are thought of as being calorie laden and full of sugar. Some favorite shades of brown are seen in chocolate, caramel, cappuccino and crème.

The artful interiors of stately homes often favor the patina of elegant antiques and polished wood floors or paneling in dark tones of mahogany and cherry woods. Burnt Sienna is a typical color of the Renaissance period. A first cousin to Brown is the lighter member of the beige family. It is generally warm and neutral and is unpretentious and classic, that which can withstand the ebb and flow of color trends. It is a safe place to begin if you have apprehensions about going too bold with color.

Variations of brown: Buff, Nude, Bisque, Ecru, Cocoa, Coffee, Cognac, Dust and Taupe

White - White in its true self is heavenly. It signifies purity. The purest of the pure, white is symbolic of peace and freedom, for example the seeds of a dandelion. It can indicate cleanliness, perfection and minimalism. It is rare to see this approach and choice in decorating because of its simplicity and cold, sterile feelings. White is more often complemented by other colors or used as the yin to the yang of black.

White walls need some type of color stimulation. Otherwise, it can cause people to develop headaches and can create a very glary and reflective space. Choosing a variation on white can lead to a much more attractive space and will create a sense of uniformity and closure, a completeness to your room. While it is true that white contains all colors of the spectrum, it is not the ideal and most desired when you are choosing a color palette for your home. Many see white as a neutral color, but without a blend of another tint or hue it appears harsh. It is far from being neutral.

Variations of White: Linen, Eggshell, Off- white, Wool, Sheer, Alabaster, Antique white, Snow, Bone and Ivory

Gray - Gray is a color for support. It is strong, yet calming and cool. A very quiet color, gray reminds us of days when we are stuck inside because of bad weather. Gray is not really a color, but is considered achromatic, or without a hue. The direct descendent of black, grays range between the darkest of charcoal to the pearliest tints. The darker tones of gray share the same feelings of black, powerful and sophisticated. Tough  modern cities are thought of as gray, cement and concrete, silvery steel and metallic aluminum. Designers use gray to depict products as sleek and high-tech. Gray is the color of intellect. Graying hair on our elders shows maturity and experience.

Moving closer to white, gray becomes more innocent and fragile. Newly birthed animals usually have gray feathers and fur, kittens, doves and the like. As gray nuzzles up to brown, it becomes warmer. It becomes associated to woodland  animals, such as a fawn or antelope. Also in stones, rocks and pebbles, birch trees and pussy willow. It is nature's most perfect neutral. Designers use it often as a background for many others because it does not clash with any other.

Though each color has a wide range of shades and tints and hues, it is easier than it may seem to choose one. Let your furniture, fabrics and other home decorations be your guide. By using what you already have, figure out what will be your focus and develop your color scheme from there.

When you have decided on a color and have narrowed down your shade options, you are ready to visit the local hardware store to pick up paint samples. If possible, bring a piece, if not all, of your focus item with you when making your paint purchase. This will ensure a proper color match. All lighting varies and what may look like one color in your living room may appear something different when you get it under fluorescent store lighting. Take the sample, along with your home decor object, outside into natural light for a second opinion.

Try to choose a paint manufacturer

that sells 1-2oz tester cans or bottles of their colors. By using these testers, you can actually paint a small portion of your wall or a piece of poster board to get an accurate idea of how a color will look. By holding or taping up that tiny paper square you brought home, you can be mislead about how that color will look covering the entire space. It is much easier to paint over a 3'x3' foot square than it is to re-paint the whole room. With good paint being rather costly, you will be glad that you took the time to use the testers. And, while you're at it, go ahead and choose two or three different shades. Light colored paint will usually appear much darker than you planned, and dark colors will show lighter.

When your color choices revolve around fabrics, use the same technique. Most retailers can provide you with fabric swatches, or allow you make a ¼ to ½ yard cut to take home and think things over. Quality fabrics can be expensive, so be sure of what you want before you buy any yardage. Like paint, once a color is mixed and a cut is made, you cannot make a return.

<u>Notes</u>

<u>Notes</u>

Making Smart Purchases for your Home

Many of us start out in our first home the same way. We have many things from our childhood room, furniture handed down from family, dishes and decorations from our last apartment or college dorm. We try our best to make it all work together. But sooner or later it no longer satisfies us. We feel the urge to create a home environment that reflects who we are as individuals, a couple or as a family. We no longer need things from our childhood bedrooms (stuffed animals and sports memorabilia); we want our home to be ours, not leftovers from the past. But where do you begin? How do you decide what to buy? What things are most important to start out with?

As a military family, you will be making many lifestyle changes and will live in many different places, homes and maybe countries. This frequent PCSing makes the challenges of purchasing things for your home even more difficult. When it comes to furniture, the possibilities are endless. Your furniture will set the room's tone; the rest of the home décor will fall into place around it. Don't be drawn into those wild and exotic, one-of-a-kinds; they can be hard to match if you ever want to add pieces at a later time. If you find something you can't resist, be sure it is of practical size and is functional, meaning it has a purpose besides being something nice to look at. Don't invest in the major trends in furniture, because just like clothing fashions, they are here today…gone tomorrow. Stick to the tried and true classics.

So, what do you buy then? How can you express your personality and make your home unique? Trendy and in-style looks can be accomplished through placing accessories throughout the home. Use fabrics, artwork, lighting and artifacts to show your style and interests.

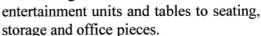

By having pieces of furniture with similar wood color, paint color and style, you can create a very modular furniture inventory. Modular means that you can separate it easily and move parts of the furniture into different areas of the house and have it look great anywhere you put it. The layout of your house and placement of the furniture will change with every house or apartment. With the main components of your room being the most flexible, your challenges of furniture placement and room functionality will be greatly decreased.

When choosing these furniture pieces, there are several characteristic things you should look for and things you should avoid. Look for pieces that can allow you to rearrange them with ease each time you relocate. Consider pieces that can be altered, folded up or extended out, to maximize your living space.

Furniture of this type can range from large entertainment units and tables to seating, storage and office pieces.

Opt for petite sofas and love seats and pair them with slipper or club chairs. Choose two love seats versus a sectional sofa. Some over-sized sofas (the kind that can double as a twin bed) can really put limits on your furniture arrangement options.

Larger upholstered living room furniture is best placed with its back close to a large wall. 'Floating' large sofas, placing them in the center of the room away from the walls, will take up a huge amount of useable floor space, leaving a minimal amount of freedom to section off other zones for additional functions, like a home office, media center or dining area. Pushing a larger sofa flush against the wall, and floating the love seat or chairs, makes for a more organized and less demanding conversation area.

Petite sofas tend to get noticed and make more of a statement when they are placed floating in a small group with other seating pieces. Smaller pieces allow for a more intimate setting and provide additional space elsewhere in the room that can accommodate bookshelves, accent tables and other room functions.

Choosing sofas and supplementary seating with smaller, less bulky arms will still afford you with optimal seating but simultaneously reduce the actual measured width of the sofa. Armless sofas are another variation in style when it comes to choosing the type of living room furniture that will best accommodate your living needs. Many pieces of armless seating can be arranged in a number of layouts and can be very user-friendly to moving military families. Although sectional style sofas are fun and provide a lot of seating space, they can be quite cumbersome when you have to move them often.

Having a variety of seating will allow you to arrange your room in a cozy and conversational way. If the furniture is so big that you have to position it far apart or against the walls or even in another room, you will generate a living room that causes family and guest separation. The purpose of the living room or family room is to bring people together, to share life stories and create memories. Chairs in these rooms should be comfortable, allowing those who sit in them to feel welcomed and encouraged to stay. Good support in the seat cushion and lumbar area are crucial for durability and comfort. More often than not, a focal point of a room can be a unique chair. Choose something that is decorative and really strikes your interest. With the rest of the furniture keeping in tradition, there is a bit of freedom and character to a chair that is dissimilar. Adding accent pillows to a simple sofa, made from similar fabric of the chair, will tie the furniture pieces together.

A coffee table and end tables are excellent ways to increase a room's storage capacity. Choosing accent tables with built in drawers and shelving will provide you with additional and decorative spaces to display or hide

items in a room that are not used regularly. A large decorative trunk can store photo albums, books and even scrap-booking supplies, providing a sturdy workspace in which to pursue your hobbies.

Ottomans and footstools are a nice addition to a living room suite. Not only do they provide an additional seating option, they are often designed with built-in storage compartments. Ottomans are great for the family room that doubles as guest room. This type of built-in space is ideal for storing the bedding that is needed for the pull-out sofa. It can also perform the duties of a coffee table, providing a nice wide surface for a tray of snacks or a game of cards. Often equipped with wheels, an ottoman can be moved easily throughout the house to accommodate your seating requirements.

Dining tables that are extendable with leaves, versus ones that are made from a single, solid piece of wood are more adaptable when fitting them into a wide range of dining areas in our homes. Having the ability to downsize your table when needed will allow better traffic flow and open up the room. A well-designed and well-crafted table may have storage space for the leaves within it, usually tucked underneath in some way. With this convenience also comes a high sticker price.

Another, cost-effective option is choosing a table with leaves, but those leaves would have to be stored elsewhere in the room or house. When storing the leaves, choose a place that will keep them from being damaged. Put them under the sofa, under a bed or even in your storage area.

Gate leg tables are very useful as well. These tables have a second pair of 'hidden' legs underneath. When the leaves are lifted from both sides of the table, the legs pivot and open out to support the table panels. Used as an accent table or sofa table when not in use, this table can serve a double duty and be added to your dining area to seat guests for dinner, a buffet of prepared food or a night of game playing.

Pedestal tables are traditional in style and are found in many dining sets from simple kitchenettes to grand dining ensembles. Having a single support leg, pedestal tables maximize the number of chairs you can position around it and no one gets stuck in an awkward arrangement with table legs. Pedestal tables are also available in extension or drop-in styles.

Dining Chairs can really add or detract from a table's function. Chairs that have arms are best placed at the ends of the table. If your dining table is on the smaller side, chairs that do not have arms will be the most

comfortable and will be easier to maneuver when trying to maximize the place settings and table space usage. Hardback or spindled chairs made of solid wood withstand the constant and everyday use in an eat-in-kitchen setting. To make the solid wood chairs more comfortable, add padded seat cushions that either tie onto the spindles or fit over the seats.

Formal chairs can be upholstered or covered with slipcovers to keep their fabrics protected from stains. Coordinate the seat fabrics with the draperies, or table linens. When purchasing new chairs, have the manufacturer add a stain-repellent such as Scotch Guard® to the fabric. This will keep the fabric from absorbing spills and allow small marks and dirt to be removed with a damp cloth.

Home entertainment units can get very large, and can cover an entire wall if they are purchased without serious thought. Go for one that, if needed, can be divided throughout the room and still serve its purpose, as well as look good.

If your living room serves as your family room and sitting room, cabinet style units that have doors that can be closed are excellent choices. While the television is not in use or you are having a quiet night with friends, you can hide all of the system's components out of view.

Entertainment units that hold and display all of your electronics are nice if you have a living room that is used mainly for watching television.

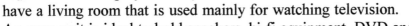

An open unit is ideal to hold speakers, hi-fi equipment, DVD and VHS components.

Keeping your video and music collections behind closed doors will keep them organized and no longer disrupt from the character of the room's design. The focus can than be directed to your accent items and the things that hold the room's look and feel together.

Lighting plays a major role in the look and feel of a room's décor. Rooms that are well-lit create a lively atmosphere and add energy to the activities that are taking place in them. A room that is poorly lit tends to be uninviting and depressing. There is a difference between a room that is poorly lit and a room that is dimly lit. Be sure to have enough lighting in a room to accent your focal items and allow family functions and entertaining activities to be enjoyed without eye-strain.

Table lamps, floor lamps and ceiling lights can be added to a room quite easily. Choose a table lamp that is smaller than the table it will be placed on. The height of the lamp should not interfere with the activities taking place or accent pieces on the table.

Floor lamps are best placed in the corner of a room where other lighting options are minimal. If a room is not wired for a chandelier or ceiling fixture, a torchiere floor lamp is ideal; opening towards the ceiling, allowing majority of the light to filter through the room. Smaller Tiffany style lamps add a lot of character and color to a space with their multi-colored glass patterns.

Let your choice of lighting fixtures compliment the mood of your area. There is a plethora of sizes, shapes and designs. Lighting is also a great way to add a unique punch of style to your home.

Simply put, smaller pieces of furniture, no matter what room they are designed for can be arranged in ways to fit virtually all living spaces. Big, bulky or deep furniture can lead to numerous problems from fitting up stairways, making it through door jams and even having enough room to walk around them once they make it into a room. I know a family that invested in beautiful new sofas before a move, only to find their next assignment put them into an apartment that was very small. Too small for their larger sofa to fit through the living room doorway. They had to leave the larger sofa in their entry hall. This was a very unfortunate situation for that family but a valuable lesson to many who visited them.

Ceiling height can frequently pose a challenge for some ornate furniture styles in many homes. Government housing units and private homes were all built at different times. Ceiling heights varied during different architectural periods, sometimes leaving eight-foot ceilings in one home and thirteen-foot ceilings in the next. When you are investing in furniture, whether it be traditional, antique or modern, stick to a height that is standard. You should be able to reach the top of the piece. On the average this height is seven feet. Many antique pieces, especially those ornate European  units, can lead to major ceiling height and room

size issues. Be aware of the details on specialty pieces. Take notice, and ask before you buy, if the base, feet, spindles and cornice work around the edges are removable. This may be necessary in a future home.

The last point to be made about purchasing furniture is QUALITY. I cannot stress this enough. Did you ever hear the phrase, "You get what you pay for"? This statement is true in the literal sense. If you take the time to save and invest in quality made, well-constructed, solid wood furniture, it will pay off in the end. Fast, fun, put-together pieces can be exciting and provide you with the immediate change you were hoping for. Unfortunately, when you go to move this type of furniture, put together with glue, wood pegs and screws, you will find the structure and quality of these items are not conducive to the moving lifestyle. Most do-it-yourself furniture projects are not made of solid wood. They are made of MDF, or Medium Density Fiberboard, which is a composite wood product similar to particleboard. It's made out of wood waste fibers glued together with resin, heat, and pressure.

Reconstituted, engineered wood products like MDF are often covered in a veneer or laminate. These thin layers of vinyl or real wood disguise the MDF, especially along visible edges. Some people prefer using MDF over regular lumber because it has a lower impact on the environment. MDF is solely made from waste products, the leftover scraps that would otherwise be dumped in a landfill. This attraction has helped it gain popularity among homeowners, however, it is not recommended for furniture pieces that are being moved often.

Over time this glue dries out and begins to break down, leaving you with

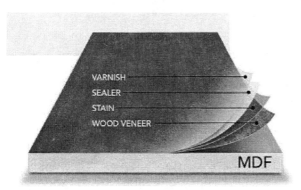

shaky and flimsy furniture. This could result in a dangerous situation. Screw holes get stripped down when you repetitively take apart and reassemble this type of furniture. Saving your money and purchasing solid wood pieces that are assembled once and remain that way during the moving process can end the cycle of buying this temporary furniture.

It's not always necessary to pay top dollar for quality furniture. Simply because something costs a lot of money, does not mean it is well made. Watch for specials, coupons and use that military discount. If you really find something you can't resist, discuss interest free payment plans or other payment options with the retailer or vendor. Don't forget about floor models. Usually they can be purchased at a discount.

Do your homework. Surf the web and see if you can find what you're looking for somewhere else less expensive. Research the product. The more you know about

what you are looking for, and the more prepared you are when you walk into a showroom, the better price you will be able to negotiate. Don't be drawn into sales pitches. Sometimes salesmen will offer discounts if you purchase more than one item at a time from them. Start slowly and don't appear desperate. They are trained to persuade you into making bigger purchases than you intended or can afford. Keep your needs and budget in check at all times. You run the show, keep the negotiating in your favor.

Thoroughly check the quality of the item. If it is a pullout sofa, open it out, lie on it, shake it (but don't damage it) and look underneath. Inspect its craftsmanship. The same rules apply for ANY new item you purchase. If a salesperson is not keen on your thorough nature, let that be a red flag, they may be hiding poor workmanship. The sales associate should be more than willing to demonstrate how items function or operate and should point out the craftsmanship and quality voluntarily.

If you like to change as the trend changes, choose items of less invested value, ones that create and provide you with the look without breaking your bank. Fabrics, pillows, candles and vases are expendable (can be easily replaced) and can be very affordable. Remember those stores mentioned earlier, where you can get brand names at discounted prices, they often carry high quality without the sticker shock. You may have to wait until you find that special something, but it will be worth the savings. When I talk about quality in home décor purchases, I am not, by any means, advising you to buy the best or the most expensive home décor items on the market, i.e. Persian carpets and

silk draperies. I am suggesting, however, that you get the best your budget allows.

For example, choose an area rug from a carpet store made of quality fibers that will withstand high traffic and can be easily cleaned. Have the carpet showroom bind the edges for you. This option can better sustain your moving lifestyle better. Your carpet will not fray and it will last longer.

Carpet is a key decorating element that you can incorporate in every room, rather easily. It is excellent for absorbing noise. It insulates your home, reduces heating costs and provides comfort over hard wood or tile floors. Carpet is certainly a vital style decision, but how it fits your room's purpose is paramount in making the right choice. A soft, short-napped wool Berber holds up to traffic and is a safe choice for most rooms, not to mention its comfort underfoot. Consider the following general information as you narrow down your search. Several factors determine a carpet's quality: how it is constructed, the pile, and the material from which it is made.

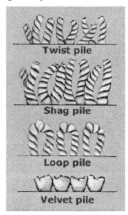

Woven carpets tend to be more costly because of their weave, while tufted and bonded varieties are the least expensive. Most household carpet is the tufted kind, which means that the yarn is stitched on a pre-woven backing.

The pile of the four main types of tufted carpets: twist pile, shag pile, loop pile, and velvet pile, is cut to different heights and often form unique designs.

Carpets that are woven will last longer than others. Flip over the carpet you are considering. Are the fibers glued onto the backing? If so, over time, this glue will break down and end up a dusty mess all over

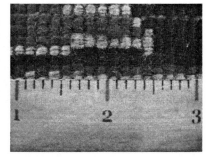

your floor. Steam cleaning your carpets will speed up this breakdown process and reduce the life of the carpet. When and where your decorating budget allows, a woven carpet is a much more advisable choice. The more knots per square inch, the tighter the weave and the better quality the rug.

When you are choosing and purchasing fabrics, it is best to visit a number of fine fabric stores first. By seeing the colors and feeling the different textures, you can learn which fabrics will give you the look you desire. When you narrow down your selection, write down the designer brand and the name of the fabric and any item numbers associated with it. Purchasing fabrics from a designer or home interior store forces you to pay several commission mark-up costs. Search around for a better bargain for the same fabric.

Use the Internet's search tools to find other stores that carry the same fabric. I've found up to a $15 difference per yard during searches. When you think you have found the best price, make your purchase. Be sure to purchase enough fabric for your project and then some extra, approximately 2 yards. Fabrics are made in dye lots and can vary slightly in color from one dye lot to the next. If you determine later that you have to purchase more fabric, you may have a color difference to deal with, not to mention an additional shipping charge. Having this additional fabric will be useful as you are dealing with different needs in each house.

There is a benefit to soliciting a fabric store in your area. The sales associates are very educated about home decorating projects and are very excited to help out eager customers. They can assist you in determining the proper measurements for a project and will be more than happy to ensure you have all the notions and proper materials needed to create professional level results. Many stores offer basic sewing classes and workshops. Consider using other fabrics that are not bought by the yard. If you are in the market for smaller quantities of fabrics, take a look at bed sheets, table linens and

thin blankets. Second-hand stores and thrift shops often carry vintage fabrics. These older fabrics are often 100% linen and a fraction of the price compared to buying them new.

Vintage linen holds a character that is unmatched in products that are on the market today. Many years ago, linen was valued for its durability and texture. Families would often hand-embroider their monogram on pillowcases, towels and table dressings.

If you are looking for a touch of something old, these linens make fine accent pillows, dresser scarves, table runners and window treatments.

So what if the monogrammed initials are not the same as your family's. See the lettering as a design rather than as someone's sentimental heirlooms. Often, the phrases and words are in a language different from your own. This makes the item even more of a unique find and a conversation piece. I have a European table scarf that I bought at a flea market, while living in Germany, that reads "Frohes Erwachsen", translated as "Happy Waking!" I find it lovely to look at and wake up to. I use it as a curtain valance in the bathroom.

Quality purchases, whether furniture, linens, dishes or accessories, present long-term benefits to you, a moving family. By starting out with better quality furniture, fabrics and accessories, you will save so much money over time. With the money you save, you can afford the next better thing that comes along.

<u>Notes</u>

<u>Notes</u>

Multi-functional Spaces
The Living room
&
Dining room

When trying to decide how to arrange all of your furniture, it is very important to take into consideration a room's shape and what activities will take place within. Most military housing offers a 'great room', or a multi-purpose room, which needs to serve as the living room, dining room and sometimes even the home office.

The room's shape usually lends itself to predict how the area will be set-up and what function it will serve. If the room is a perfect rectangle, you will be faced with challenges of room separation or room cohesion. An L-shaped room tends to separate itself, naturally defining a line between the end of one area and the beginning of the next. Whichever situation you are presented, there are countless solutions to what normally would be considered a decorating dilemma.

Getting creative and allowing your mind to develop solutions to your problems is only the first step. Initially you may have to think untraditionally and find uses for household items other than what they are intended for. Start by keeping it real and keeping it simple. There is such a thing as being too creative.

When you are given a room of this sort to deal with, the first step is to keep all of the items in the room flowing together. Use similar color schemes and styles, and choose related textures and fabrics. This creates a very natural flow between areas, blending them into one multi-functional and useful space. Although this sounds effortless and beautiful, it is sometimes difficult to create this atmosphere when you are trying to use what you already have. Most of us are faced with the challenge of putting together a room with various styles and patterns. If you are just beginning your military moving adventure, or are considering replacing that hand-me-down furniture with things representing your own personal style, now would be a good time to do so. Let go of the worn out, eccentric and dated pieces, and replace them with neutral or traditional items. The job of combining furniture and accessories will be much easier. Make small changes through accessories and accent pieces, and your room will not only appear neat and organized all the time but it will be functional too.

It is best to determine the activities that will take place in the room before placing the furniture and designating your "zones". Take into consideration the socializing aspect and the overall flow of traffic. Can guests or family members easily communicate within the room or are everyone's backs toward each other? Can you walk from the living space to the dining space avoiding obstacles? Can you focus on computer work while others are watching the television?

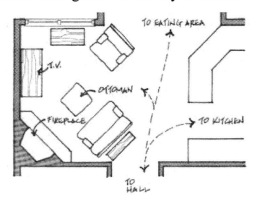

Once you place the main furniture in the ideal position, add the smaller pieces around. The main pieces of furniture are the sofas, dining table and chairs, entertainment units, china hutches, and shelving. Enter the room from every possible direction. If there are any sharp angles or things you must maneuver around, then it is necessary to make some adjustments. Move from one functional space to the next, placing the smaller things as the end tables and coffee table, planters and fixtures in areas best suited for them.

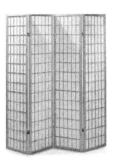

The second way to use the open floor plan is to divide the room into several different areas. Use room dividers, screens, curtains and other things you may have available to section off one zone from the next. Arrange the furniture in a way that would separate the spaces preventing one room from opening into another. Using the back of the sofa to make a division is very common. Place a narrow table behind the sofa for use as a small buffet or tabletop space in the dining area.

Another popular room divider is an open backed shelving unit. Choose an

open unit that is finished on both sides and is attractive when viewed from either living space. It acts as a wall, while still allowing light to flow through and conversations to be heard, yet keeping the functional areas separated and defined. It can also display items related to both functional areas.

Fabric used as curtains to divide space adds a wonderful textural element to a room's décor. It acts as a focal point in a large room and can be very helpful in controlling noise. Fabric absorbs sound, so the more fabric you have in a room, from pillows to drapery, the quieter and cozier your room will be. Attaching a curtain to a rod, suspended from the ceiling, is advisable. Opened the curtain when you intend to invite the flow throughout the entire room or draw it closed when privacy is preferred. There are many types of curtain rods and attachments to meet your individual needs.

A popular example is a system of wires and clips that can be attached to the walls and pulled taut, close to ceiling, virtually unnoticeable.

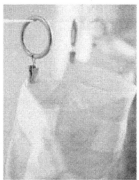

Observe the placement of the windows when determining the room's layout. Before you install a divider or curtain, be sure that you are not blocking the natural light entering through a window or doorway. Natural light is important to the overall feeling and the energy flow of a room. If you must block a window, choose a transparent fabric that will allow the light to pass through, but still act as a wall between the two areas.

Whether you are beginning with an open floor plan or closed, making initial purchases or using what you have, keep in mind that you are not living permanently yet. If you purchase everything to match and coordinate with your present housing situation, you may be separating it later into several rooms. Having all your pieces looking exactly alike can lead to a very ordinary living space. Neutral pieces and matching pieces are not necessarily the same thing. Mentioned earlier, by choosing pieces that are neutral, you will be able to use them in a variety of locations throughout your home, as you need them. Matching pieces, ones that are exactly the same color shape finish and style, are not going to add the unique character to a room that you may be looking for.

Colors and patterns are crucial when it comes to successfully separating or dividing a room. Even though each functional space or zone, as they have been called, is completely different in pattern, style and color, you can make them eye-pleasing and complimentary when seen altogether. Perhaps you need to remove, or temporarily eliminate, all the patterned objects. Too many contrasting pillows, cushions, blankets, curtains and knick-knacks can be over-whelming. Discover the room's limit regarding the number of patterns you will introduce. If you have three different colors, one in each zone, you may need to merely bring back the object or objects that compliment those colors. Change some stripes and plaids to solids, or vice versa. Too much visible clutter can also transform a rather simple room into one that appears disorderly.

Floor coverings can play a great role in the overall appearance of an open floor plan. If possible, try to keep the floor coverings within the same color family. By having bold and contrasting colors on the floors of each area, you create a  distraction to the overall cohesion of the room and the smooth shift from one zone to the next will be interrupted. Keeping the floor coverings analogous is a wonderful way to blend a space together that has many differently styled furniture pieces and color choices. All flooring options do not have to be the same materials, just the same tone. You can have a beige carpet in the living room, pinewood flooring in the dining area and white linoleum in the kitchen and they will still work for each other, instead of against. This follows the similar concept of choosing neutral linens.

On the other hand, when you have very neutral and matching furniture with a minimal amount of color throughout the room, your flooring can play the opposite role by separating one zone from the other. By choosing more drastic floor coverings (oriental rugs, animal skins and patterned carpets), separate areas are clearly defined. Place them appropriately in each space. Center a small rug within your living area, another under a dining table. Be sure to have something else in the zone complimenting your choice of flooring. A piece of art on the coffee table or bold colored pillows and accessories create unity and encourage the eye to make distinctions between your functional areas.

Dressing the windows in a multi-functional room can sometimes lead to the curtains you already own fitting the window on the opposite side of the room from its coordinating furniture. If this is the case, try to dress the windows in the main part of the room first. If the living room area takes up the majority of the room, use those window treatments first. If there are more windows than curtains, or they are the wrong size, then it may be necessary to purchase new or additional panels.

Choose a curtain or panel that will work in a number of your rooms. Stay away from bold and colorful prints. Subdued prints and light colors are the best. Curtain panels can be hung on a variety of different rods and are designed with different looks to work with any décor. Because paneled curtains are rather simple in style, choosing curtains with a unique hanging method can change the look and add a little flair to a room. Get straight standard panels, in the longest length possible. This gives you length to experiment with tie-back and styling options.

A standard rod pocket will cover the rod and allow the fabric to gather, creating a ruffled and full look. If the fabric you choose is flat in texture and plain or solid in color, a standard rod pocket can create depth and character to your window treatment.

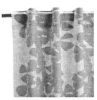

A hidden pocket will also cover the rod completely and will cause the fabric to gather in deep opposing folds. Fabric that is decorated with a large print can handle this pocket style well. When the curtain is in the open position, the gathering is minimal and the pattern of the fabric is not distorted.

Tab-top panels expose the curtain rod almost in its entirety. A more decorative rod system should be used when choosing this style of panel. It becomes part of the character and design of the window treatment. Fabric options range greatly with this style and should complement the rod you choose.

Eyelet curtain panels take on a look all their own. A thin metal rod system is ideal and should match the eyelet material. Minimal gathering occurs with this type of curtain choice and can support heavy fabric like corduroy and denim. This curtain style is great for a room that is in need of a masculine touch.

Sheer fabric panels can work wonders and can be purchased in pocket styles similar to solid fabric panels. Sheer fabrics filter harsh sunlight yet at the same time allows natural light to enter a room. Fabric is available in a very big assortment, from prints to stripes and even in a vast array of colors.

Because curtain panels hang straight to the floor, you can dress them up with tie-backs or trims. There are unlimited ways to bunch and gather panels that are too long or too wide. Curtains need to be as multi-functional as the room itself. They may serve a completely different need in the next place you live. Tips, techniques and steps are outlined for these quick fix methods in 'You Can Do-It-Yourself', beginning on page 185.

Curtain holders are mounted to the wall, next to the window frame. Rather than drawing the curtains all the way open along the rod, by simply sweeping the panels behind the holders, you can change the look of your window treatments. Holders should match the rods to complete the overall appearance of the style.

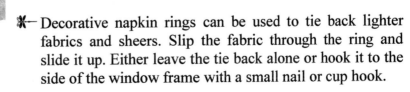

Decorative napkin rings can be used to tie back lighter fabrics and sheers. Slip the fabric through the ring and slide it up. Either leave the tie back alone or hook it to the side of the window frame with a small nail or cup hook.

✳— Tassel tie-backs come in various widths and sizes and can be used not only for draperies but added to chair backs, table runners and the corners of full size table cloths. Tassel clips attached to window shades can spruce up an existing window treatment or a window that is covered by only the shade itself.

✳— Clip-on earrings, belonging to a set of costume jewelry, work just as well. Thrift shops, yard sales and second hand shops usually have a wide selection of these items.

Whether a minimalist or a materialist, your open floor plan can work for you. With a little imagination and a lot of determination, you can have the rooms of your dreams, every move you make.

Living room areas are used by families for many different reasons. The functions of this room include entertainment, reading, and game playing. Often the living room is converted into a guest room containing a pull-out sofa. No matter what the activity, in order for this room to accommodate everyone's needs organization needs to be established.

Begin your organization project with the '**Ten Minute Tidy**' rapid sorting task. In order for the '**3-box-method**' of organizing to work the way it should, all items in the room need to be accessible and grouped together, like things with like. Leave the large furniture pieces for later since they most likely will be staying in the room.

Once you have sorted through every cabinet, box, bag and drawer, you should have before you piles that need to be further divided in one of the three boxes labeled **Keep, Sell/Donate** and **Discard**. Use the following lists as recommendations and a place to begin the process.

✓ Games with all the pieces ✓ VHS and DVD films that you watch repeatedly ✓ Throw blankets and accent pillows ✓ Books and magazines you read often ✓ Photo albums and scrapbooks ✓ Entertainment system remotes and accessories ✓ Room Decor you enjoy displaying ✓ Candles and lighting elements ✓ Entertainment serving pieces you use often ✓ Storage bins and containers that work	✓ VHS tapes and DVDs you no longer view or the children are too old for ✓ Gently used blankets and pillows ✓ Gently used furniture you no longer like or that has been replaced ✓ Music CDs that have been copied to your computers hard drive ✓ Books you will never read again ✓ Knick Knacks you no longer have interest in ✓ Small furniture pieces that only provide a look and not a function, it is taking up space	✓ Games with missing pieces ✓ Home recorded television shows on VHS cassettes ✓ Old books, and past issue magazines and newspapers ✓ Candles that are close to being finished ✓ Duplicate remotes that come with entertainment system components ✓ Photos that are blurry or uninteresting ✓ CD jewel cases ✓ Worn or pilled blankets and pillows

The Dining room is often a room that is not used on a regular basis. When a home is designed with an 'eat-in' option in the kitchen, the dining room typically becomes reserved for entertaining friends and family visitors. Meanwhile, the room sits there collecting dust waiting for that special occasion.

Dining room buffets, cabinets and breakfronts are usually filled with the overflow of dishes from the kitchen, table linens, and china place settings and are frequently loaded with entertaining decorations and serving pieces. Many of these items seldom see the light of day. The space being occupied by 'special' things may be of better use if your formal items were minimized.

Be realistic when you begin to organize and decorate this space. Most of the items you will find have not been used since the day they were unpacked and put away. It is also possible that some of these things haven't been used during the last few moves. More often than not, there are sentimental attachments to many of these objects.

Wedding and Anniversary gifts probably make up the majority of the formal pieces. Although it is difficult to part with memories, it is more difficult to relocate these memories when they take up space and never get used.

Apply the same principles you have been using throughout this book thus far to organize and de-clutter your dining area. Begin the 'Ten Minute Tidy' sorting process here. Remember to get everything out of the cabinets, drawers and buffet. Work quickly and efficiently. Try not to think too hard about why you should keep an item or why you should not. Go with your initial instincts, they are usually the right ones. This is not the time to get sentimental. Focus on what you use and what you don't. You can decide what to do with the unused items later. The following lists will get you started and on your way to a fabulous dining room.

✓ Place settings and formal serving pieces ✓ Table linens with proper measurements for your table ✓ Good lighting fixtures ✓ Candle holders and accent pieces you often display ✓ Art work or photographs ✓ Napkin rings and place cards	✓ Table linens that are not the right size for your table ✓ Odd and end dishes that do not match the rest of your collection ✓ Candle votives and holders you seldom use ✓ Extra utensils not belonging to a set ✓ Napkin rings you no longer use ✓ Duplicate crystal dishes and bowls	✓ Broken or cracked dishes ✓ Faded, worn or stained table linens and placemats ✓ Vases and bowls from floral shop bouquets ✓ Damaged or un-repairable furnishings and lighting fixtures ✓ Taper candles less than 4 inches long

Because the dining room is generally a simplistic space, additions of focal elements and color schemes can transform this area into one that deserves attention. When that special occasion arises and you adorn the formal table with your favorite collections and accents, the room will come alive.

The dining room can be the perfect place to establish a home office, when no other space is available.

❈— A side table or accent table makes a quaint home office space.

❈— Use space in a cabinet or buffet to store office supplies.

<u>Notes</u>

The Living room: Floor Planning Template

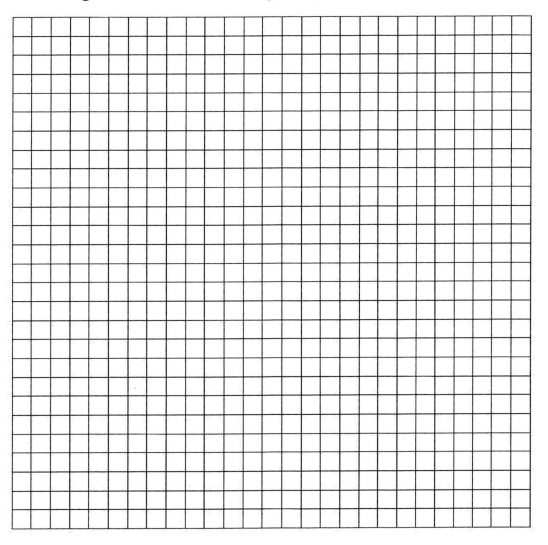

The Dining room: Floor Planning Template

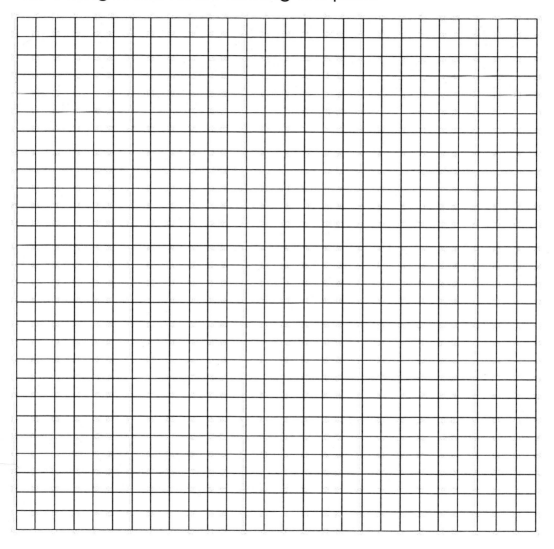

The Kitchen

Often referred to as 'The Heart of the Home", the kitchen is the central room where your family's daily activities begin and end. From your morning coffee and breakfast routine, school preparations and work scheduling to your dining in the evening and possibly a midnight snack, the kitchen is where it all happens.

The kitchen is also the main communication center of the home. It is imperative that this area functions efficiently and that all actions have their defined zones. Some of these zones include:

- Food Preparation
- Dishwashing and Storage
- Cooking
- Food Storage
- Home Office Center
- Dining Area

When you are determining zones, it is important to keep related activities within close proximity of the supplies needed to perform them. The Food Preparation area should revolve around the refrigerator and the pantry. Kitchen plans that are designed with an island in the center automatically provide a food preparation zone. Your spices, oils and similar ingredients should be easily reached. Also in this are should be your preparation tools such as knives, measuring spoons and cups, cutting board, bowls and dishes for serving. Food preparation appliances such as a food processor, blender and mixer are best located in cabinets below the counter.

If your kitchen is not equipped with an island, it is possible to purchase an island for this function. A portable island, usually on caster wheels, is a great addition to any floor plan that can accommodate one. Available in many varieties, with open shelving and closed, with butcher block tops and drawers there is a style to match any room décor and kitchen preparation needs.

If your kitchen space does not allow for an island to be added, chose an area of the counter to designate as the Food Preparation zone.

The dishwasher is typically installed under a section of the counter next to the sink. This naturally provides you with your Dishwashing and Dish Storage zone. The cabinets located above the dishwasher should house your daily serving pieces. The drawers next to the dishwasher are ideal for your flatware and serving utensils. To determine the appropriate Dishwashing and Dish Storing zone, stand in front of your dishwasher as if you are unloading. You should be able to remove clean items from the dishwasher and put them in their storage places without moving throughout the room. This zone makes the daily chores of setting the table and washing the dishes easy. The space under the sink should hold dish towels, detergent and basic cleaning supplies.

Cooking for yourself and your family is one of the greatest gifts you can give to those you love. Making nutritional choices that create healthy and wholesome people is invaluable. Holding conversations around the dinner table about your daily activities is only complimented by a good meal.

Entertaining friends usually revolves around sharing a meal of some sort. Whether it is a pot-luck buffet or a more formal sit-down style occasion, food is always a focus of the event.

In order for your cooking experiences to be successful, timeliness of preparations and accessibility to pots, pans, potholders and utensils is crucial. The Cooking zone should revolve around the oven or stove. The drawers and cabinets closest to these appliances should hold cooking necessities.

Storing your food items requires a space of its own. Non-perishable items, canned goods, un-opened boxes, refrigerator and freezer items are all included in this Food Storage zone. These things should be kept in cabinets or pantry close to the refrigerator and freezer. Keeping all of your major food ingredients together will allow you to know exactly what you have and will eliminate the need to impulse buy when you can't find the ingredient you are looking for. Food purchased in bulk quantities should be put into a storage space outside of the kitchen. When needed, bringing a few items at a time into your food storage zone will create space for a wider variety of food products. This will enable you to experiment with new recipes because you will have a larger selection of ingredients to choose from.

Because the kitchen is typically the main communication center in the home, it is necessary to establish a Home Office center, even if your home allows for a formal office space. A home office center acts somewhat like a satellite location. Here you can keep track of daily activities without having to continuously trek back and forth from the kitchen to the office every time a schedule changes or a telephone number is needed.

A corner of the counter, a small table in the entry or even a drawer in the kitchen can provide just enough space for this. Included in this space should be the telephone, a small file system to hold school papers, incoming/outgoing mail and a small assortment of desk supplies.

At the end of the day or the close of the week, sort through the mail, gather your receipts, balance your bank accounts and file your paperwork. Move all of the contents into your main office area and organize them into the proper paper system. If you have not established this paper filing system, then you should put that task on the top of your to-do list. The system you create in your Home Office will directly affect the organization and time management of your day.

Lastly, your kitchen may accommodate a table and chair set or even a breakfast bar with a few stools. This eating area should remain free of paper clutter, appliances and dishes and be an open, welcoming space for your family and guests to relax and unwind.

In order for your kitchen functions to run smoothly, it is essential that clutter is non-existent and that every item kept in this space is used regularly. Initially performing a quick '**Ten Minute Tidy**' will provide you the opportunity to evaluate your kitchen goods and afford you the chance to set up your new kitchen zones.

After you have sorted your belongings, distribute the items into one of the three boxes of the '**3-box-method**' of organizing. The following is a list to assist you in determining which items are to be placed in which box.

✓ Complete sets of silverware ✓ Complete sets of dishes ✓ Working utensils ✓ Fresh ingredients ✓ Updated appliances ✓ Sharp knives ✓ Pots & pans ✓ Clean plastic storage containers ✓ Casserole dishes ✓ Wine glasses ✓ Measuring utensils ✓ Unstained dish towels ✓ Serving dishes you enjoy using ✓ Baking sheets and cake pans that are in good non-stick condition	✓ Mismatched mugs ✓ Item you no longer use or do not match your décor ✓ Fancy appliances you rarely use (waffle maker, popcorn popper) ✓ Old cookbooks you no longer reference ✓ Placemats and cloth napkins you no longer use ✓ Canister sets ✓ Efficient appliance you have upgraded ✓ Duplicate trash cans, buckets, mops and brooms ✓ Odd knives and utensils ✓ Mismatched serving pieces and dishes	✓ Old spices (over 1yr.) ✓ Old vinegars and seasoned oils ✓ Expired foods ✓ Sticky bottles and containers ✓ Burnt or peeling pots & pans ✓ Stained dish towels ✓ Broken appliances ✓ Old mop heads and sponges ✓ Old vitamins ✓ Very used cutting boards with deep cuts ✓ Soiled carpets ✓ Plastic containers with missing lids or bottoms ✓ Spoiled food in fridge ✓ Freezer burned or unidentified foods in freezer

Decorating your kitchen takes a minimal amount of effort and money. A few simple accents on the windows and walls can turn your kitchen into a chef's delight. There are many products and organizing solutions available that will help keep your functional zones in working order.

Your kitchen cabinets are high on the priority list when it comes to organizing your dishes, glasses and other meal time equipment. To get the maximum space out of your cabinets, the addition of portable adjustable shelving may be necessary. These free-standing shelves make it possible to store various sized plates, bowls and glasses without stacking them too high.

Flatware and other eating and serving utensils can get over-whelming and over-looked when placed in drawers. The use of utensil organizers is a great idea, but the sizes of drawers vary so much in each home that

it seem inevitable that the one you currently use will not fit in your next kitchen. Drawer organizers are available in several varieties, as adjustable

trays that expand when desired or as individual, modular trays that can be arranged in drawers as needed.

The space under shelves can also be conformed to hold your wine glasses and mugs. Using small cup hooks that screw into the underside of shelves or a mounted wine glass holder can free up space on the shelves for other dishes and serving pieces. The addition of a spice rack on the inside of the cabinet door also increases the required shelf space for larger and heavier kitchen items.

When placing your dishes into the cabinets, each type of dish should have its own stack. Placing too many unmatched dishes on top of one another creates difficulty when trying to retrieve one particular sized dish from the bottom of the pile. This awkward maneuver initiates a greater potential for others to be dropped onto the floor and broken.

Glasses should be lined up in columns from the front to the back of the shelf with similar dimensions. Doing so will keep the hunt for the correct glass at bay. Line up the tall glasses, the short glasses and then the tumbler or juice glasses. Although souvenir glasses, mason jars and character cups are fun to drink from and remind you of a special event, they rarely do justice to  your kitchen when you are trying to achieve a space that is uniform, organized and functional. Those extra drinkware items should be used for the moment and then eliminated from your kitchen space. Store them in the drink cooler if they are your designated 'outdoor/ picnic/ party' glasses.

Pots and pans are best placed in the drawer beneath your oven. If your oven does not have this built-in storage or your collection is large, the use of an overhead pot rack may be the best solution.

* Hang the pot rack from the ceiling over an island or over your sink. As soon as you wash them, hang them to dry.
* Attach a peg board with hooks to the wall next to the stove and hang your pots and pans accordingly.

Every family has different needs when it comes to deciding on the appropriate type of home office or message center. Depending on how many members are in your family, their ages and the amount of activities each participates in can, contribute to the amount of detail your message center needs.

* A family calendar is advantageous for the busy household. Family members can each be responsible for updating their individual activities on a regular basis

* A message center that hangs on the wall and includes a cork board, calendar and a space for notes is great positioned in an entry way, on a pantry door or by the telephone. This type of center is ideal if your kitchen counter space is limited.

* A simple chalkboard can be a very affordable and helpful scheduling tool for the family with a minimally confusing schedule. Use the chalk board to write phone messages, shopping lists and reminders. Just erase them when finished. This eliminates the paper clutter and the search for lost notes and loose memos. Add a decorative frame to an ordinary chalkboard and create a piece of art for your kitchen wall. Use as a wine list or menu when you entertain.

* Replace two of your kitchen table chairs with a bench. This will slightly increase your seating. Another option is a padded bench with additional storage, good for kitchen items that are not frequently used but necessary. Coordinate the cushion fabric with your window treatment.

* Replace large electric appliances with smaller handheld versions. Replace the food processor with a chopper, the slice toaster if you have a toaster oven and the electric can opener with a hand turned opener. Eliminating the bulky appliances will create space for other functional needs.

* Use cloth napkins for a valance over the kitchen window. Change them with the seasons for added accents. Experiment with folding and ironing to create unique patterns and lengths. Add coordinating placemats to the table, make chair covers or cushions with the matching table cloth or two cloth napkins sewn together and filled with a 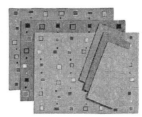 pillow form. Choose a basic sewing technique described in the final section, 'You CAN Do-It-Yourself'.(pg. 196)

* A free-standing cabinet or sideboard provides added storage in a larger kitchen space. Add decorative knobs and pulls to the cabinets. Replace built-in doors handles and drawer pulls with matching hardware for a uniform and cohesive look. Choose a piece without knobs for a modern,, sleek look.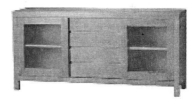

* Add a fun and funky wall clock in the kitchen. With all of the scheduling and time management happening here, wouldn't it be great to love the clock you look at?

* Choose plain, yet decorative, soap dispensers, oil bottles, towel holders,  utensil jars and canisters that contain items that must be out on the countertop. Keep your counters clear of clutter and available for cooking and you may be more likely to take more time in food preparations rather than costly take-out meals and frozen dinners.

With all of the kitchen zones in full function, the daily activities that take place within it will become smoother and more controllable. The morning stresses and our hurried ways will soon be replaced with peaceful, cheery mornings and calm well-organized schedules.

Make your kitchen a place you enjoy being. Surround yourself with delicious foods and healthy ingredients. Take the time at meals to sit with your spouse or family and share thoughts, concerns and stories of your day and your life. Be thankful for each other and celebrate together all the wonderful experiences being a military family has offered you.

Check out the new food guide pyramid at www.mypyramid.gov for the latest updates and research on maintaining a healthy lifestyle.

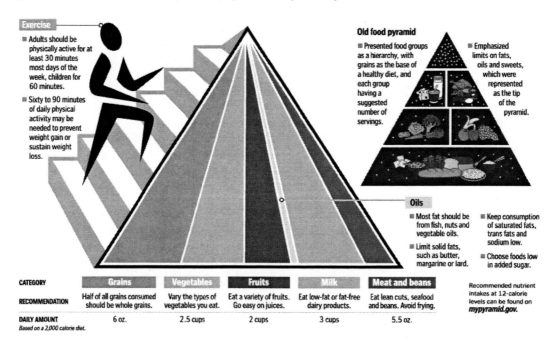

Exercise
- Adults should be physically active for at least 30 minutes most days of the week, children for 60 minutes.
- Sixty to 90 minutes of daily physical activity may be needed to prevent weight gain or sustain weight loss.

Old food pyramid
- Presented food groups as a hierarchy, with grains as the base of a healthy diet, and each group having a suggested number of servings.
- Emphasized limits on fats, oils and sweets, which were represented as the tip of the pyramid.

Oils
- Most fat should be from fish, nuts and vegetable oils.
- Limit solid fats, such as butter, margarine or lard.
- Keep consumption of saturated fats, trans fats and sodium low.
- Choose foods low in added sugar.

CATEGORY	Grains	Vegetables	Fruits	Milk	Meat and beans
RECOMMENDATION	Half of all grains consumed should be whole grains.	Vary the types of vegetables you eat.	Eat a variety of fruits. Go easy on juices.	Eat low-fat or fat-free dairy products.	Eat lean cuts, seafood and beans. Avoid frying.
DAILY AMOUNT	6 oz.	2.5 cups	2 cups	3 cups	5.5 oz.

Based on a 2,000 calorie diet.

Recommended nutrient intakes at 12-calorie levels can be found on *mypyramid.gov.*

<u>Notes</u>

The Kitchen: Floor Planning Template

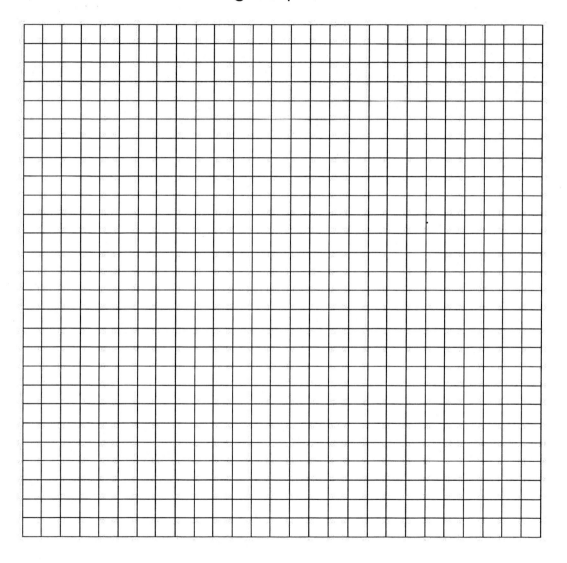

The Master Bedroom
&
Guest Room

The master bedroom and guest room seem to be the last on the list when it comes to organizing, decorating and relocating. Maybe it is because we can 'shut the door' to those areas. Is it out of sight, out of mind? Or is it…out of sight, constantly on your mind? Rooms other than the living room, dining room and kitchen can simply be avoided when we go about our daily routine or even while entertaining. Maybe you figure that not much happens in those spaces and with your eyes closed, while you sleep, you can't even see the clutter. Well, these rooms and spaces are just as important as all the others. You will sleep better, entertain easier and find things faster…therefore making your whole life more productive and stress free if these rooms are not neglected.

The furniture pieces in these rooms are usually basic and standard. Most of the decorative items are accents and extras; life's little pleasures. The functional purposes in these rooms are clearly defined and practically the same for everyone. The bedroom is where you are supposed to find rest and relaxation, while freeing your mind of your 'to do' lists and becoming physically and mentally prepared to begin a new day. If the room stays clutter-free, this freedom will be much easier to accomplish. Maybe your family routine involves all cuddling up in the master bed while you watch a Friday night movie, or it's the place to slip away and indulge yourself in a nightcap or lounge about feasting on your favorite take-out. Whatever your bedroom habits are, they deserve a special place in which to occur.

The bedroom is a private space to take you away from the daily grind of working, cleaning, cooking and child rearing. What are the excuses for letting this area get out of control? Is it time? Money? Space? Whatever the reason, the end effect brings you to the same place, right in the middle of clutter.

Consider the master bedroom and guest room (if you are lucky enough to have one). In it is a bed, a dresser or two and possibly nightstands and a closet. The rest of the bits and  pieces are for looks, not for function. Bed linens will fit the bed no matter where you put it. Your clothes will find their usual place in the dressers and closets

and your curtains go on the windows. So why do these rooms so easily get crammed with boxes, clothes, books, toys, extra furniture, strange things under the bed and storage tucked in the back of the closet? Simply put, because we have lost sight of the purpose of the bedroom. We have taken all of the things that make us uncomfortable and edgy from the living areas of the home and slowly accumulated them where no one can see them. Now, you lay down in your bed to rest after a long day, surrounded by the clutter and blinding reminders of the disorganization in your life, job and family, and are expected to get a good night's sleep.

The decorating industry recognizes the importance of your bedroom space and has taken a huge marketing plunge into providing you with all the necessary merchandise to fulfill all of your wildest dreams. Notice the large trend in Bed & Bath issues of popular mail-order (and internet order) catalogs.

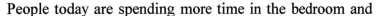

People today are spending more time in the bedroom and more money on the things they choose to fill it with, than they have ever done before. High thread count sheets, big plush throw pillows and billowing rich draperies are only some of the specialty items within your  reach, and the "click of a mouse". Consumers are spending so much money that these companies are designating entire issues on the subject of decorating and designing that perfect bedroom getaway.

So here's what you need to do to get yours. Let's begin in the master bedroom with the primary focus being on creating a retreat, a place filled with the things that bring you joy and pleasure. Your time is spent doing so much for the others in your life, a spouse, child, boss or another family member. Now it is time to do something special for yourself. The project of the master bedroom and guest room can be accomplished in a matter of a few days, depending on the amount of time you have to dedicate to this task each day, on the current condition of your room and the extent of the changes you want to make. In a short amount of time, your life can take a turn for the better. Having a single place to call your own works wonders by eliminating the day-to-day stresses of life.

Begin your project by determining what is essential to the room's function and what is not. Try to think about what you have versus what you need. Do you know that most people only utilize 20% of what they own? That means we hold onto 80% of our household goods for "later" or "to use in the next house". Making a serious effort to liberate our home environment and rid our rooms of unnecessary clutter will make the job of becoming organized and maintaining that system more manageable.

Apply the '**3-box-method**' of organizing to your master or guest bedroom. Begin by grouping all similar items together. Quickly and efficiently box up all items from the room into one of the three categories, **Keep**, **Sell/Donate** and **Discard**.

✓ Clothing, shoes and accessories that fit and are in style ✓ Family jewelry and photographs ✓ Books still of personal interest ✓ Sturdy furniture ✓ Accent pieces such as picture frames, candles and art work ✓ Suitable lighting fixtures ✓ Seasonal blankets, pillows and window treatments	✓ Name brand clothes that no longer fit but are still current ✓ Working electronics ✓ Jewelry of value and quality ✓ Name brand shoes or handbags ✓ Slightly used blankets or linens ✓ Furniture you no longer desire ✓ Gift items you received but no longer care for	✓ Books and magazines you will never read again ✓ Worn or stained bed linens ✓ Clothes that are worn or out of style ✓ Beauty products that are older than 6 months ✓ Stockings with runs and stretched elastic ✓ Knick- Knacks that have no personal value

Once the majority of items have been sorted, and the '**3-box-method**' is accomplished, completely empty the room (closet too!). Put everything that was in the **Discard** box into the trash, the **Sell/Donate** items should go into storage until a later date, and the **Keep** items can be moved into another room or the hallway for the time being. The only items remaining should be the bed with its frame and furnishings, the dressers and any small nightstands or chairs. Larger furniture pieces are too heavy to move yourself. With everything else out of the room, they can easily be slid around and placed out of the way and then into their new location. When sliding furniture, especially on hardwood floors, place a small square of cloth or carpet under each corner or leg to prevent scratching the floor's surface.

Take all the items out of the room that are in the drawers or on shelves. Take the pictures off the walls and curtains off the windows. Clean the room, top to bottom. Wipe out the closet, drawers and shelves, wash the windowsills and windows, launder the curtains, and any bedding. The room should appear to be much larger. Appreciate the space and try not to let too much come back in to take away from that feeling. If you would like to change the paint color, now is the time. Steps to painting a room are clearly explained on page 187.

Arrange the furniture in a way that allows good movement throughout the room. Walk in and out of the room numerous times to see if there are any adjustments that need to be made, once you have it all in place. According to the ancient, time-honored tradition of Feng Shui, translated in Chinese meaning "wind and water", there is a proper way to arrange your home in order to  acquire the best energy, or ch'i, from the earth. It is the 'balance' and 'harmony' that we create that directly affects our lives and emotions. To most, it sounds a bit weird, and I thought so at first too. But when I learned about its history and conducted a few "studies" of my own, I began to see those balances and feel the energy. Now every time I am decorating a room, I try to incorporate some of the techniques. Take it or leave it, I have found that there is a truth to the furniture placement in the bedroom. If not done for the Chinese tradition, it is a good place to begin. There are many books available on the market about this Feng Shui technique. Before you invest in another book, check your local library and the Internet for more theories behind this Chinese tradition.

⬥ The bed (head) should be against the wall. If the bed is not touching the wall the person may be unsettled and not sleep soundly. There should be equal distance next to both sides of the bed.

⬥ The bed should be placed in a position that the person lying in it can see anyone coming through the door. Ideally, it should be placed as near as possible to the corner that is diagonally opposite the door. However, our lifestyle is far from what most consider being ideal and we know that these options are not always feasible. In the end, the bed should wind up where it best fits and where it creates a good feeling upon entering the room.

Lay on the bed. What do you see? Is there a nice view out the window? Are you looking at yourself in a mirror? A nice view of outside is good, a view of yourself getting out of bed…well, maybe not so nice.

⬥ The dressers should be placed in the room next on walls not already occupied by the bed. Keep them slightly separated from each other.

⬥ Try not to have all the furniture pieces lined up.

⬥ Since getting dressed usually involves articles in your closet as well as your dresser, place the dressers within close range of the closet.

⬥ Reposition the bedside tables and follow with other furniture that belongs in the bedroom suite. Nightstands with drawers or shelving can keep books or writing supplies handy.

⬥ Bring in any lighting. Small bedside lamps are a good idea for the avid nighttime reader.

⬥ Position and re-hang pictures and mirrors back on the wall, their placement may need to be changed if you have moved around the furniture.

◈ Mirrors should be hung where they will reflect the natural light of the window or door. When standing in front of the mirror, you should see a window in the reflection. If when lying on the bed, you cannot see the door, a mirror should be placed in a position that would allow you to do so. If there are numerous mirrors in a room, none of them should reflect the other. This will cause the energy and focus to just bounce around the room without stopping. Bad Ch'i!

◈ Re-hang the curtains and redress the bed.

The next task is the most difficult of all. Initially, only bring back into the room the accessories, clothing and accents that you favor. Position the key elements of the room where they are seen upon entering the room. Make sure these are items that you use regularly. Once your drawers are shy of being full and your closet starts to get the slightest bit crammed...STOP. You have reached the point of maximum capacity. In order for your room to remain clutter-free and organized, and retain that peaceful and sobering environment, you have to know when to call it quits.

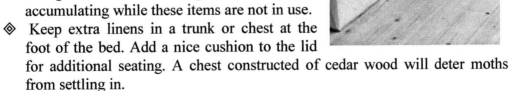

◈ Utilize the space under the bed by storing off-season clothing in shallow bins or zippered cloth bags Space allowing, these bins can be equipped with small wheels, or casters to aide in their retrieval. Keep your under-the-bed storage closed; this will prevent dust from accumulating while these items are not in use.

◈ Keep extra linens in a trunk or chest at the foot of the bed. Add a nice cushion to the lid for additional seating. A chest constructed of cedar wood will deter moths from settling in.

◈ Extra dressers or closed shelving units can be used for the overflow of clothing if your closet space is limited.

◈ Adding a window seat, with storage within, provides that extra space for

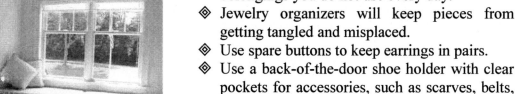

belongings you do not use every day.

◈ Jewelry organizers will keep pieces from getting tangled and misplaced.

◈ Use spare buttons to keep earrings in pairs.

◈ Use a back-of-the-door shoe holder with clear pockets for accessories, such as scarves, belts, lingerie and ties.

◈ When labeling containers that will be visible, place the label on the side or inside edge rather than the front.

Clothes closets in the bedroom are usually rather small for the amount of things that need to be stored in them. In most circumstances, the master bedroom has one closet that must be divided and conquered by two people. Take time to reduce the amount of clothing you own. The **Keep** box, bag or pile of clothing you have made, following the '**3-box-method**' activity, will most likely require additional purging. Try these ideas to assist you in narrowing down your wardrobe:

◈ Replace all wire hangers with proper and sturdy wooden or plastic types. Appropriate hangers for shirts and pants will make finding articles much easier.

◈ Color-code your hangers. You and your spouse will then see who the bigger closet hound is.

◈ Once your clothes are hung properly, tie a piece of ribbon to a hanger and place it at one end of the clothes rod. Each time you wear something, return it to the closet but hang it on the other side of the ribbon. This will give you an idea of which garments get worn most often. Give this method from 1 to 2 months and then eliminate the clothes you do not choose to wear.

Maximize the amount of space a closet has to offer by making a few, rather simple, adjustments to the rod placement and possible shelving. Here are a few ideas that may work for you:

◈ Add another rod behind the existing rod for occasionally worn clothing if your closet is deep.

◈ Replace a side-to-side rod with front-to-back rods for a closet in which the door is centered with deep spaces on both sides.

◈ Replace rods with shelves or add a bookcase or shelving unit into the closet. Add hanging shelves that Velcro® over the rod.

◈ Lower the clothes rod and add a shelf or two above it.

◈ Hang long garments to one side and shorter items to the other and place a small dresser into the closet under the short garments.

◈ Utilize the door for ties, belts and shoes.

◈ Add an additional closet to a room with a system of curtain rods mounted onto the ceiling. Hang draperies that coordinate with your room's décor.(Great way to hide an office space located in the bedroom)

I realize stopping at this point will leave you with quite a bit that was taken out that will not be going back in. You may have to make further decisions about selling, donating or discarding those leftovers. Going back to the '3-box-method' of organizing, you will find it not only easy but rewarding as well when you have found new homes for all the extras you no longer have to live with or rummage through every time you enter your new relaxing retreat….Ahhhh…Rest well!

Applying the same technique to the guest bedroom will eliminate the habit of using that extra space as storage. When guests enter a space you have designated for use during their stay, they should have complete freedom to make themselves at

home in that room. How do you think a guest would feel if they went to hang a few items in the closet to find it jampacked with your stuff? What if they open drawers to find your extra clothes or storage items? That would not create a welcoming impression. Think back to your experiences in other guest rooms. What elements of those rooms seemed to make you the most comfortable or made you feel least welcome?

Guest rooms should be clean and crisp. The color scheme should be neutral and pleasing to everyone. The closets and drawers should provide ample space for your guests to unpack. If necessary, these drawers and the closet can hold extra towels or blankets. A decorative dish or bowl is a

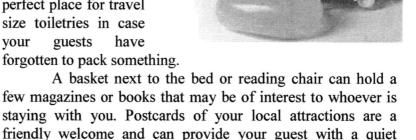

perfect place for travel size toiletries in case your guests have forgotten to pack something.

A basket next to the bed or reading chair can hold a few magazines or books that may be of interest to whoever is staying with you. Postcards of your local attractions are a friendly welcome and can provide your guest with a quiet moment they may not get at home, to write to a family member or friend. The items in this room should be useful to the person or people using it. If your guest room will be accommodating small children, have some children's books or movies easily available for them to borrow during their stay. There is nothing more awkward than for a guest to have a need and not know where to find it. This room is their getaway, their retreat, a place for them to be removed from their daily obligations and focus on making their time with you and your family unique and special.

Place a personalized touch in the room that will let your guest know that you have really gone out of your way to make their visit with you a memorable one. If you have photos of their family, a photo of you in somebody's company or a memory of a vacation you spent together, put them on the dresser or nightstand. Hang a mirror on the door or wall and place an alarm clock and a lamp next to the bed.

Purchase a small blank guest book or scrapbook and a  one of kind pen in the nightstand drawer. On the last day of their trip, encourage your guests to write about their holiday. You will then have a collective journal of your visiting friends and family. Later you can add photos that were taken and any correspondence of thanks received after their departure to the journal for a finished and organized memory book.

As a test, spend a night or two in that room as a guest would. This will help you to create the perfect environment for those you care about.

<u>Notes</u>

The Master Bedroom: Floor Planning Template

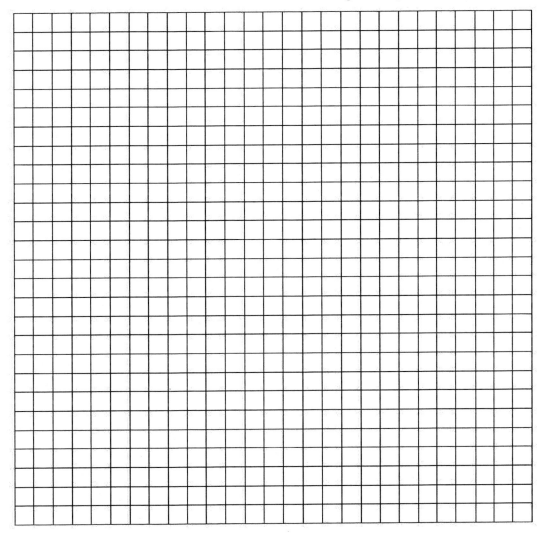

The Guest Room: Floor Planning Template

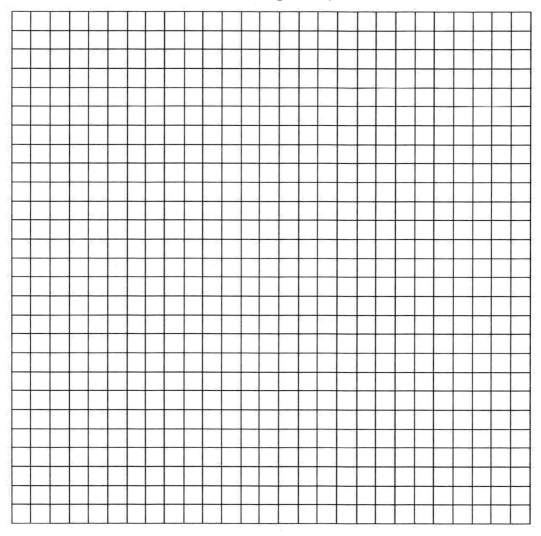

The Bathrooms
&
Closets

I believe that a bathroom should be kept very clean and tidy. It is a room needing daily attention and upkeep in order for dirt and mess not to take over. Used by all family members, it can be a haven for germs and bacteria. Keeping the bathroom in order and eliminating all the extras, will allow the space to be user-friendlier.

Creating that spa like feel in the bathroom will generate a space that everyone will enjoy. Simple storage systems are a practical way to keep each family member's belongings together and out of the way of everyone else's.

Start by quickly sorting all of the bathroom items into piles, one for each family member. Stick to the rapid **'Ten Minute Tidy'**. This will help you determine the amount of storage space each person needs.

Begin your bathroom transformation with the same approach laid out for you regarding organizing the bedroom. Start with the '**3-box-method**' of organizing. Sorting and emptying the room completely.

✓ Towels and linens in good condition and those in sets ✓ Unopened accessories (i.e. toothbrushes, deodorant, dental floss) ✓ Shelving or furniture for decoration or storage ✓ Shampoos, bubble baths and similar products that are your desired brands ✓ Cold remedies that are not expired ✓ Cleaning supplies	✓ Fabric shower curtains ✓ Extra towels in good condition no longer favorites ✓ Unopened bath and body products and gift sets ✓ Duplicate blow dryers, curling irons and other appliances ✓ Gently worn bath robes ✓ Containers and sink accessories that have accumulated from past organizing attempts	✓ Expired medications ✓ Make-up and beauty products over 6 months old ✓ Worn out, torn or fraying towels ✓ Orthopedic braces, wraps and accessories from past injuries ✓ Rusty toiletry accessories (i.e. tweezers and nail clippers) ✓ Old rolled up tubes of creams and ointments ✓ Old toothbrushes and razor accessories

Clean the walls, floors, and medicine cabinets. Empty the closets and wash all the linens. Once the bathroom has been disinfected and polished to a shine, you can decide on any changes that you will be making and complete those projects before returning anything back into the room.

After the bathroom has been freshly painted (with a semi-gloss variety), or not, you will have to evaluate what will go back in and how will it fit best.

O   Medications are not effective if they are old. For safety purposes, flush any unused portions down the toilet. If the items have not been used within the timeframe they were prescribed, dispose of them too.

O   Beauty regimen products like make-up and skin care can harbor bacteria due to the continual contact with our eyes, lips and skin. After six months, these items should be tossed.

O   When you are replacing any medicinal items back into the room, be sure they are placed in a medicine cabinet or on a shelf, out of reach of small children. If necessary, place these high-risk items in a locked cabinet or child-proof container.

Measure the size of the closet shelves or cabinet that will store your family member's new containers. If each person has their own system, the whole function of the room will improve. When it is your turn in the bathroom, wouldn't it be great not have to pick up after the last person before you are able to begin your daily routine. If you were to enter the bathroom and find it clear and clean and ready for you, time will be saved and energy will be reserved for more important things.

Don't forget about the walls and shelves in the closet. This space can take on a look all its own. Paint the shelves and walls of the closet in a color that is fresh and bright. Let the color you choose be complimentary to the accent pieces you are going to put elsewhere around the room.

- **O** If the room can support the look, take off the door to the closet so its new organizational systems are exposed. Not only will this look fabulous, it will also encourage everyone to keep the area neat and clean.

- **O** If the shelving will be exposed to the room, make the selection of baskets, plastic bins or cloth covered boxes uniform in shape and size and neutral colors, like white or cream. When they are seen altogether in the closet or on the shelves they will give the appearance of that clean and crisp spa.

- **O** To differentiate between owners, hang a luggage tag or small ornamentation off the handle or apply a label or sticker to the front of the container with the owner's name, choosing fancy character fonts to dress them up a bit.

The accessories in the bathroom should be uniform in color and style. Bathroom fixtures and storage containers should be made of plastic, stainless steel or washable fabric. It is important to be able to disinfect these items regularly. Neatness is key here. Most bathrooms are too small to support a variety of styles and an abundance of decorations. It is important to maintain the purpose of this room. It is a place to groom and pamper yourself. By relaxing in a warm bath, applying spa treatments to your skin and nails, or spending some time alone, this room should be enjoyable. If bold and crazy assorted colored towels, children's bath toys, and the clutter of everyone's varieties of beauty products surrounds us, then how are we suppose to feel relaxed and refreshed?

○ A rolling cart with a number of shallow drawers will keep smaller items like nail polish, band-aides and make-up from getting lost. Multi-colored drawers can coordinate with each family member's 'bathroom color'. Easily wheeled in and out of a closet and into position for use, this caddy will eliminate any mix-ups and clutter.

In a smaller bathroom, the shower area should have a shower curtain that is not too busy pattern-wise or have too many colors. A curtain in a small space should blend into the look and feel of the other walls. By using a soft, solid fabric, like terry cloth or waffle-weave, the attention will not be drawn to the tub or

shower stall. Shower curtains with delicate and simple trim can also be used here. This will keep the room light and spacious, making it look larger than what it is. A larger bathroom can support a shower curtain with a pattern or print, but still keeping the colors light as to not take away from the overall style that is being portrayed. Hooks for hanging shower curtains can be very decorative and add a unique touch to a basic shower curtain. Adorned with gems, flowers, balls and icons, there is sure to be a set that will match your bathroom's look.

In addition to the manufactured hooks, you can utilize some items you may have elsewhere in you home. Try beaded bracelets from children's party favors or Mardi Gras parades. You can also buy these bracelets in trendy, yet inexpensive, jewelry shops in the mall. Bracelets with a clasp work best; just thread the bracelet through the holes in the shower curtain and clasp over the rod.

Fabric stores and craft store are stocked with thousands of spools of decorative ribbon. You may have ribbon stashed away with your gift wrapping supplies or sewing notions. Cutting pieces of ribbon and tying your shower curtain to the rod, adds pizzazz to a bathroom. If you change the style or color of your bathroom, it is very inexpensive to change the ribbon too.

If your bathroom allows for a bold curtain, keep the hooks plain and simple, they will be lost in the pattern of the fabric so there is no need to invest in fancy hooks. The standard plastic rings or the stainless steel roller rings are ideal. Be creative and try anything once. The worst thing that can happen is it won't work. Just keep in mind that however you choose to decorate

your bathroom, consider how it will look in bathrooms to come.

Shampoos, conditioners, soaps and other hygiene items should be kept off the sides of the tub. You can easily and inexpensively find wire racks or suction style shelves to hold these products, and keep them hidden in the shower area behind the curtain or door.

Hanging shower caddies are hooked over the shower head and remain within reach for all your shower needs. By leaving items sitting on the side of the tub, enclosed in a damp environment, moisture builds and molds can rapidly grow. Keeping the sides of the tub and shower stall clear will make the chore of cleaning and disinfecting more attainable so it is completed more often.

The edge or countertop surrounding the sink should hold nothing more than hand soap and a small hand towel. If you do not have a medicine cabinet and must leave your toothbrush, cup, cotton balls and personal hygiene items out in view, be sure they are in matching containers and accessories.

These accessories will add cohesion to all the smaller things that can sometimes make a space appear cluttered, even thought it is really not. If you have small children, a plastic variety of these accessories will withstand the occasional drops into the sink and onto the floor.

O Adding a candle or small vase of flowers can promote that spa-like feel.

O Hairdryers, brushes, toothpaste and deodorants should be kept beneath the sink or in the medicine closet.

O Items like cotton swabs, facial tissues and mouthwash, which are .used by everyone, are best kept in small containers or mason jars on a shelf or window ledge.

What about all of those lotions, body washes and beauty sets you get as gifts, but never seem to use? Most of the products in these collections are very high in alcohol, which dries out the skin. They are not typically made solely of natural and

organic oils but artificial fragrances and dyes, made to mask odor rather than remove it. Using bath products that are good and nourishing for your skin, made of natural ingredients, honestly clean you without the perfumes. Although a little more expensive, natural products last longer and can be used in less quantity. Those fancy colorful bottles may look nice sitting around, but manage to make it through every move unused. Pass these along or dispose of them.

Towels in the bathroom seem to multiply. They fill up the towel bars and then tend to be draped over the doors and handles, especially if there are a large number of family members using the same bathroom.

○ Designating one wall hook for each person can help in determining who used which towel last, and will eliminate the need to get a new one every 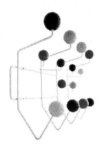 time you shower. If your bathroom does not allow space for everyone's hooks, one on the back of each bedroom door will do the trick. This also reduces the amount of laundry that comes from the bathroom. Towels are very bulky and washing them unnecessarily can do damage to the electric and water bills. Hint: Use the same identifying marker from the containers to signify whose hook is whose, or designate a 'bathroom' color to each person. Mom's towels, hooks and bins are white…Dad's are beige. The number of towels a bathroom should have is two times the number of people who use it. If there are five people in the family, then ten towels need to be available. There should be one for the moment and one on-call for when the other is being laundered. That's it!

○ A large basket of toilet tissue next to the commode will keep plenty of rolls handy and eliminate the hunt at an indisposed time. Bathtub toys for  the children are best kept in a mesh bag hanging in the closet or behind the door. Other storage options can be a bucket or basket. Again, be sure they are dry before tucking them away. Toys should be run through the dishwasher often to break down the soap accumulation, kill germs and prevent mold growth. A little bleach in a sink of hot water will also work as a disinfectant.

As mentioned previously, when purchasing towels, rugs and curtains for the bathroom it is better to choose quality over quantity. Good, absorbent 100% cotton towels will last a long time; neutral colors will always remain 'in', and never go out of style. Keeping them traditional in color, they are bound to match every bathroom décor. Add a personal accent to towels with a family monogram. Any local embroiderer will be able to offer you a selection of fonts and colors to choose from that will turn plain towels into custom luxuries. Hand-sew a decorative trim across the bottom of your towels that coordinates with you bathroom accessories.

Use a basic back stitch to attach the trim (step-by-step instructions are provided in 'You CAN Do-It-Yourself' on page 207). As your bathroom colors and tastes change from house to house, you can easily remove the trim and add a different one. Pom-pom, gimp and tassel fringe are only a few possibilities to choose from. Visit a fabric store or craft store to see more options. Accents, like small dishes, candles and flowers make it easy to add a focus color and are affordable to replace when the trend changes or you just need something new to look at.

- Pom-pom trim, available in numerous sizes.

- Gimp trim, also unlimited possibilities.

- Jacquard ribbon, adds lots of color and style.

- Tassel fringe, in various lengths and materials.

Closets in the halls and bathrooms will also hold extra linens and household items. Be sure when putting things away in closets they remain within close proximity of their functional area or zone. Avoid filling closets with too many items from all over the house. This "all-purpose" style closet makes it difficult to keep each interest separated. Eliminating the need to search for things when you need them will save you time and stress. Bed linens should be stored in the bathroom or hall closets, close to where they are going to be needed.

O Label the shelves if the items are not containerized such as sheets, blankets and towels.

✻— When storing bed sheet sets, fold the fitted sheet, flat sheet and one pillowcase in a neat and uniform size. Insert them into the remaining pillowcase, and fold under. This technique will keep you from searching for matching pieces. Do the same for bedspreads and shams. Stacking the sets or dividing the shelves by size (twin, full, etc.) will take the guesswork out of locating the linens you need.

One of the most difficult items to fold correctly and neatly is a fitted bed sheet. Thanks to Target®, you will never wonder how it's done, ever again. Here's how:

❖ Hold the sheet inside out, by its two adjacent corners on one of the shorter ends. Position your hands inside each of these two corners.

❖ Fold the corner in your right hand over to the corner in your left, enveloping it. With your right hand, pick up the corner that is hanging down in front and fold it over the two corners in your left hand.

so far, so good.

❖ Pick up the last corner and fold it over the other three corners. The sheet should now be right side out.

❖ Place your folded sheet on a table and straighten it, tucking in the elastic edges as you go.

❖ Fold the sheet into a rectangle and then again until it is the size you require.

How neat is that!

Voila! 100% perfectly folded fitted sheets...

O Table linens are best stored on hangers. Gravity will keep the wrinkles out of the fabric and they will be in ready-to-use condition. If you have a variety of sizes, place a hangtag or label on the hook of the hanger with the dimensions and a  brief description of the cloth (i.e. 24"W x 48"L, white lace). When returning the laundered cloth to the closet, you will be sure there is a designated place every time, by the hanger labeled for it. Keep smaller doilies and handkerchiefs folded in a pile.

Additional closets throughout the house should be task efficient. Closets should not really be used for long-term storage, unless you have no other option. Household items that are not used regularly are best kept in the attic, basement or alternative storage areas. Closets in the living areas of the home should remain designated for items needed for the everyday function of the room without the visible clutter.

 Smaller items that need to be stored in a closet (sewing notions, batteries, photos or candles) can be kept in decorative hatboxes or other containers and will look tasteful and organized when stacked on a shelf or on the floor. Small jars, candle votives or canisters will help disguise the appearance of all the bits and pieces. A personal favorite way to store small things is in VHS/photo boxes that you can get just about anywhere. Available in craft and office supply stores, to department and franchised stores, they are the ideal solution to storing an abundance of things. They are a perfect size for almost anything and come with a small frame on the side in which a piece of paper is easily slid in to keep them all labeled. Available in prints suitable to everyone, and fitting in any room's décor, they are very attractive. Labels can be changed out as needed. Use them as gift boxes and the recipient will get two gifts in one.

O   Install a shelf above the bathroom door or around the ceiling for additional storage. Mount the shelf approximately 2' from the ceiling. Add a thin piece of crown molding on the underside of the shelf, where it would be seen. On these shelves place baskets or bins holding duplicate toiletries and extra towels. Roll the towels and stack them in a pyramid

pattern for that unique spa look. Shadow box cubbies add character and can be mounted to walls in a grid pattern or randomly where needed.

O   Attach a fabric skirt around a pedestal or free standing sink to create additional storage space. Use one of the sewing techniques in the 'You CAN Do-It-Yourself' section of the book. Attach the skirt to the sink with double-sided Velcro®.

O   Add an accent piece of furniture to a larger bathroom for a cozy and personal touch. Original antique furniture or a collection of pieces is very appealing.

O   Store cotton balls, swabs, band-aids and small manicure accessories in clear canning jars.

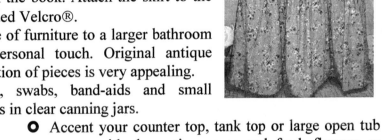

O   Accent your counter top, tank top or large open tub corner with decorative vases and fresh flowers or greenery. Bathrooms focus around cleansing and purifying. Plants clean the air we breathe and can add vitality to your newly organized and de-cluttered space.

Let your mind free itself from daily worries while you indulge your senses in your newly decorated space.

<u>Notes</u>

The Bathroom: Floor Planning Template

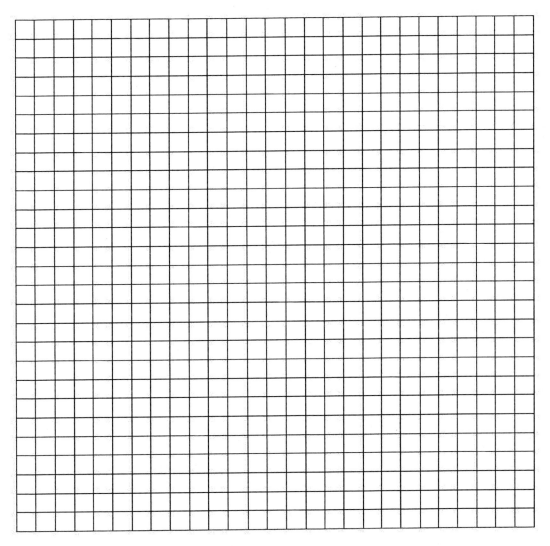

A Child's Room

More activities take place in a child's room than any other room in the house. It has to accommodate their play, sleep, schooling and entertainment of friends, as well as be that little quiet space to call their own. Unfortunately, children's interests change as fast as their wardrobe does and what they wanted yesterday isn't even close to what they want today. They grow at lightning speed and their little toddler toys are soon replaced by larger entertainment systems.

Throughout that rapid cycle of life, many adjustments constantly need to be made to the way their room looks and the purpose it serves. These changes are often costly and parents wind up feeling frustrated, wondering if another investment in their child's room is the right financial decision. Why can't we get it right? Why does it always seem that when we think they have all they need, they are ready for more?

Fortunately for parents, the major furniture pieces in their rooms do not need to be replaced as often as their tennis shoes. From the moment a child is born, their room is equipped with a crib, changing table, dresser and even a shelf for books and toys. As the child grows, the crib is replaced with a "grown-up" bed and a desk takes the place of the changer.

By the age of three, most children's rooms are filled with mix-n-match furniture, an assortment of toy storage systems and an abundance of decorative artwork. We seem to get our children's room to this point and then become comfortable with it because it "works".

When a parent is questioned about which room in their house needs the most organization or redecoration, the usual response is their children's rooms. Why is it that we can have such an interest and pay close attention to the way our living rooms, bedrooms, bathrooms and closets look and are kept, but when it comes to our children's rooms we put it on the back burner? Maybe we assume they will not take care of the nicer things until they are older. We figure they are just going to ruin it all so why bother buying it.

We expect them to keep their clothes folded in drawers, their toys put away and their rooms in tip-top shape on their own. The number one chore a parent gives a child is to clean their room. We teach our children to pick up after themselves, so one day they can be neat and orderly grown ups. How are we suppose to teach them about organization and decorating if we overload their personal space with too many clothes, too many toys and way too many frivolous gadgets and then not give them enough space to store it and the means to take care of it all?

As an adult and a parent, we control what comes into the house and what goes out. It is typically our money that buys the things to fill our children's rooms. So let it be our responsibility to set some sort of a standard when it comes to determining how much is too much and when to say "no".

Starting from scratch would be easy. We would make smart choices for furniture, storage and decorations. To begin with an empty room and an unlimited budget would be ideal. 99% of the time, however, that is not the case (if we could only be so lucky). We usually decide to make a drastic change to our child's room long after it has passed the point of no return. And we get frustrated with our children for not maintaining the environment we created for them.

Approaching the task of organizing and decorating a child's room takes patience and time. It may cost us a bit more, but when completed we can end up with a very functional and manageable space, one that a child can maintain more easily and will enjoy spending time in.

Smaller children, under the age of 6, usually get excited about having something new. They are used to change and enjoy the surprises that come along with it. Older children, on average, are against the idea and express that their room is their personal space and may be more reluctant to make drastic changes. Sit with your child and discuss with them the concept of making adjustments to their room. If they are resistant from the get go, offer to put most of the new decorating choices into their hands. For example, if you give them the opportunity to decide on the color and the style, you may have more control over the final outcome than they will realize (i.e. you let them choose blue as a new wall color…you determine the shade of blue that gets purchased).

Before plans are developed and purchases are made, initial decisions have to happen regarding what things are going to be kept and what items are no longer used or needed by the child. Give a child one task at a time, and be there to help them along the way. Turn the project tasks into quality time with your child, which is so hard to come by under normal circumstances these days. When boredom sets, but before tempers flare, call it a day. Arguing is counter-productive and may lead to the end of a project before it begins.

Start off sorting through their clothes with the '**Ten Minute Tidy**'. Younger children may like to do this in the form of a fashion show. They will know immediately which clothing items to let go of because they won't be able to get them on. They will reach for their favorites first and will start to loose interest in the 'game' once the special things have been tried, and the not so

favorites begin to emerge. Use this breaking point as a guide to which clothes you can remove from their wardrobe without a fitting session, preferably when they are not around.

An older child may prefer privacy when trying on clothes. If your child is a "clothes hog", a little bit of bribing can work wonders. Offer them one new shirt for every five they no longer wear or volunteer to donate. Some older children don't really get caught up in the latest fashion trends and may have clothes in the bottom of their drawers or in their closets that they out-grew years ago. They could care less about what they wear or how often they have worn it. All it usually takes for these children to cooperate is a generous offer to help them with the decisions.

Once their clothes have been sorted and the ones they are keeping are neatly returned to their proper places, they should appreciate the work they have done and will realize that this organization project may be cool after all. Replace all of the mixed and matched hangers with new hangers that are uniform in color and shape. A few decorative hangers for their special garments will encourage children to keep up the organization.

Using the '**3-Box-Method**' once again, decide which items need to be placed in the three boxes or bags labeled **Keep**, **Sell/Donate** or **Discard**. Younger children really enjoy this rapid activity. Besides having an otherwise time-consuming task completed in ten minutes, it is also finished within the average attention span of a child. You and your child will make instinctive decisions rather than allowing time for sentiment and negotiating to take place. Listen to your child during this process. Children tend to be a bit more honest about which toys they like and which ones they use. If you, as the parent feel otherwise about a particular item, put these toys into storage until you can let them go. Use the following lists to get started.

✓ Age appropriate books	✓ Games with all pieces	✓ Broken toys
✓ Age appropriate games and toys	✓ Clothes in good condition	✓ Dolls with missing limbs
✓ Clothes that fit and are in good condition	✓ Art work	✓ Used up art supplies
✓ Art supplies in good condition	✓ Out-grown books	✓ Games with missing pieces
✓ Linens used on a regular basis	✓ Out-grown sports equipment	✓ Torn books
✓ Music listened to regularly	✓ Out-grown videos and electronics	✓ Clothes with holes, stains or stretched elastic
✓ Age appropriate furniture	✓ Baby equipment	✓ Balls that won't inflate
✓ Age appropriate artwork	✓ Fast food trinkets still in packaging	✓ Fast food trinkets
	✓ Games and toys that were gifts and unopened	✓ Cracked or broken storage bins
		✓ School papers and old workbooks

Toys and other personal belongings seem to accumulate out of nowhere. We pick them up a little treat while out shopping, family and friends send token gifts of love and the flow of presents that enter their lives between birthdays and holidays is never-ending. These trinkets and gifts are totally unavoidable and can rarely be returned. What happens to them is sad. Unless they are something the child had really asked for, they magically find a way to get crammed into every bin, drawer and empty space possible, never to be played with again.

Try to eliminate those "filler" toys from your child's collection. Reduce the amount to extra art supplies, books that are for a younger child and fast food prizes. If they are still in good condition, but there are just too many, put the extras away and pull them out from time to time to replace the used supplies with the fresh ones. Keep desk supplies separated in plastic bathroom caddies.

Let a day or two go by between tasks. Children can get overwhelmed when they are given too many things to do at one time. They may not be able to share your excitement and vision of what the room will look like when it is finally finished. By spreading the projects out over a period of a week or two, your child will not seem pressured and feel their space is being invaded.

Once you have completed the sorting and eliminating phases of the project, look at the organization phase. What type of organization system will best suit the items your child has to accommodate? Do they need a large bookshelf, with matching colorful bins to keep their belongings separated? Do they need a wardrobe with doors to close up their eclectic and mismatched possessions? Maybe a few narrow wall shelves to hold their delicate collectables.

Determining the type of storage that will best suit your child is often decided by the ability of the child to keep the room maintained, once the project is complete.

Each age group has different needs and therefore will need different zones to maximize the space in their room. Nurseries belonging to infants are more for the convenience of the parent than for the use of the child. There should be areas set up for sleeping and changing, as well as playtime on the floor. Bookshelves can hold stuffed animals and new treasures and gifts from family and friends.

A toddler or small child needs the most organization and most defined zones. They need a place for games, books, crafts, costumes and toys along with an area for getting dressed and keeping their clothes in order. Because a child's clothes hang rather high in a closet, the dresser may be moved into the closet as well to open up some much needed floor space. Once the child's hanging clothes reach the top of the dresser, it will have to be removed from the closet. By this time a child has most likely decreased the amount of zones they require and the space will allow for another piece of furniture.

Teens and young adults have very few needs and their number of zones significantly decreases as they age. The time they spend in their room is mainly for schoolwork and entertainment. Teenagers need areas designated for work, music, entertainment (video games and television) and a little bit of storage for their childhood toys.

Investing in good, quality storage systems will allow the child to grow with their room's design with a minimal amount of investments. Flimsy and cheaply manufactured storage bins and shelving will need to be replaced often. The most economical decision you can make when decorating a child's room is to choose sturdy and simple pieces. Containers and bins with handles and lids that fasten will make cleaning up and organizing more enjoyable and attainable.

Deep storage systems are great for the bulky stuffed animals and dress-up costumes, hats and accessories. Once the child has outgrown the toddler phase, toy boxes and trunks made ideal storage systems for coloring books, craft supplies, photo albums or extra pillows and blankets for overnight guests.

The primary pieces of furniture in a child's room should be fun but functional. Children should want to spend time alone in there as well as feel good about having in friends. Keeping the core furniture colors neutral, like natural wood or solid white will provide you with freedom to make many and

affordable changes as your child grows. Trundle style or day bed frames are perfect for a growing child. They both come with the option of housing another bed or a drawer system underneath the main bed. Day beds can also double as extra seating, perfect for your teenage child's lifestyle.

Color and style can be added to the room with the addition of curtains, bedding sets and artwork. Garlands of flowers and strings of colorful lights make a simple bed into a magical fantasy space. Choose fabrics that are of traditional colors and patterns. Fabrics with varying textures and fibers can add a lot of character to a room without being too dramatic. Stick with one color scheme and avoid popular characters and prints. The novelty and interest of that retro, circular print bedspread may wear off before the fibers wear out. If your child insists on the fun and trendy look, choose a few non-permanent ways to achieve it.

❖ Place an accent area rug by the bed or use it in a corner to section off a reading zone, an art zone or a lounging area. Choose several rugs with the same colors. If the primary rug is bold and colorful, the secondary rugs are best solid or slightly textured.

❖ A wall hanging, or fun design painted onto artist's canvas can add a lot of style and really set the mood of a room. A child can do this themselves or you can purchase a print to compliment the room's décor. It is not always necessary to choose the traditional framed pictures and art to decorate a wall in a child's room.

❖ There are many accent items that can be hung or adhered to a wall to dress up a room. Large wall stickers can be purchased that add polka dots, stripes and even theme images to a blank space. These stickers are very affordable and can even be removed and reused. Add them to closet doors, window shades, mirrors and vinyl shower curtains.

❖ Punch holes in the corners of vinyl placemats and hook them together with ribbon or binder clips. This makes a very hip drape and allows plenty of privacy as well as light to come through the window.

❖ Contact paper can be used to create a color block effect or a wide stripe around the room that compliments the fabrics and accessories. Use it to add multi-stripes to the lower half of a room; cut the contact paper in strips, varying the widths and apply to walls in a pattern or random arrangement. Use several colors in the same monochromatic scheme or use contrasting colors for a bolder affect. Contact paper can also be cut to cover the fronts of drawers, the tops of tables or even cardboard boxes when making your own organizing containers. Wallpaper is another option if you want to add design and a unique character to storage bins or room décor.

❖ Change the hardware on the dressers, doors and drawers to add emphasis and bring some style to traditional and simple furniture. There is an unlimited variety of knobs available. Check your hardware stores along with the major mass-market competitors.

❖ Large floor pillows and beanbag chairs can make the bed or floor a perfect spot for reading or watching television. Pile several pillows in a corner and add a mesh canopy to the ceiling for a whimsical retreat. Fun and colorful beanbag chairs add drama and excitement to a child's space.

❖ Spruce up plain and solid colored curtains by adding a necklace, beads, trims, scarves and in-style hair accessories. Tie them back, bunch them up or clip them on.

❖ Label toy bins with laminated photos of what belongs where for the little ones who can't read. Color-code the bins or drawers, add different colored knobs or even tie ribbon to the handles to help toddlers learn their colors (i.e. Put the trucks in the blue drawer).

❖ Paint your child's name or an inspirational quote in large letters above the bed or dresser.

❖ Tie lengths of ribbon on a rod with coordinating room colors.

❖ Add a decorative wall paper border around the top or center of the room. HINT!! Coat the pasted side with spray starch and adhere to wall. When you are ready to move…just peel it off.

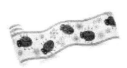

❖ Hang fun paper lanterns from the ceiling over the bed. Buy or make them using balloons and paper mache.

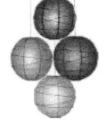

❖ Use groovy door curtains as room dividers for a shared room.

❖ Attach drawer pulls or decorative hooks to the footboard or window sill for extra hanging space.

Most importantly, keep an area in the room designated for free play. Children need to make a mess; it is part of the learning process. Allow them to have that independence, but also give them the means to clean up the mess after they are finished creating it. Have a comical clean-up routine to encourage your child to keep their room organized. Make up a catchy jingle to sing while you clean. A fun clock can lend a hand in teaching your child time while you accomplish tasks.

Using bins, boxes and labels (photos if the child is too young to read) to give all items a space, they find ease in the chore of cleaning their room and will be more cooperative when you ask them to do so.

I have a friend who received many toys from her mother-in-law, which were once played with by her husband as a child. How special those children were to be given that treat of sharing their father's childhood pleasures. Especially in a family whose current military lifestyle does not allow their parents such an opportunity to hold onto to many of their children's memories in material things. But the days came when their children were no longer interested in these old-fashioned toys. They wanted the fun stuff that all the other kids had. So, as any parent would do, the toys went into the closet, onto the top shelf, to stay. As other toys found their way into the children's room, the room began to slowly run out of space. Despite feeling bad about taking up room that could be used for other things, my friend still could not seem to part with her husband's hand-me-downs. A suggestion I made to her seemed to make matters easier. My advice was to box up those toys and send them back to her mother-in-law, along with a beautiful and heartfelt note of her deep appreciation and

expression of thanks for the use of the toys, at the same time explaining that as the children have grown, their interest in those toys have grown old too.

Children show more responsibility in keeping their own rooms neat when they are the ones making the decisions about what to keep, what to get rid of and where it all belongs. If your child's room is over-full and cluttered, the task of keeping it clean is virtually impossible. There needs to be a place for everything. Each toy should have its own shelf; each article of clothing should have a place in a drawer or hanger in the closet.

When they have more than what they can accommodate, they find difficulty in organizing it all.

In today's fast paced and manipulative market, we have to consider how much is needed versus how much is wanted. By limiting our children to only having what they need, and on a truly special occasion what they want we eliminate the over-spending and over-cluttering of their rooms and lives.

Notes

A Child's Room: Floor Planning Template

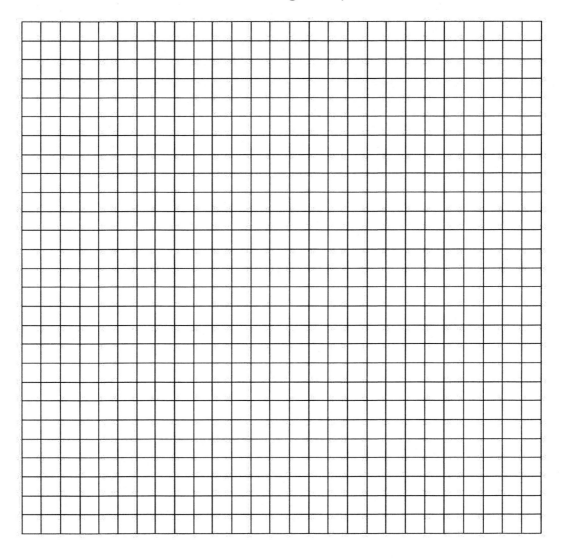

The Home Office

When it comes to designating an area in your home for use as a home office or study, be certain to consider who will use the space, how often the space is utilized and how much space you require for the furniture and accessories you have.

Location, Location, Location! It is imperative that you set up your office in an area in the home that is, if possible, secluded from the hustle and bustle of life. Very important work is accomplished in this space, your home finances, study time, work related tasks, and correspondence. All of which are best completed under calm and rather quiet circumstances.

If you are not fortunate enough to have a complete room to use as an office there are many other small nook style places in a home that meet most office needs. A corner, the end of a hallway or a landing can make a great workspace. If you are using a computer, printer, telephone or fax machine in the space, keep in mind all the wires that will have to be concealed.

Tech junkies would encourage you to "go wireless". If you can afford the new wireless technology, you will find that choosing an office area will be much easier. Not having to rely on the phone jacks and Cable or DSL hook ups, being within cord reach, your options for setting up shop are limitless.

If you do however, need to have all the wires running all over the house, use proper and fire safe methods to mount and disguise your electrical jumble. Using a staple gun to attach wires to the baseboards isn't the best way. If you accidentally staple through the cord you are creating a vulnerable area for an electrical spark.

Fancy hardware stores and electronic stores may try to sell you expensive gadgets and new-fangled products. Use these stores for the product names and ideas, and then find a better bargain in a mass-market chain somewhere else. I have actually used the cardboard paper towel and empty bathroom tissue rolls to keep my wires neatly bundled together. If your wires are visible, use twist ties, Velcro® straps or zip-ties to hold them secure and tidy. If your needs exceed your limits, call in a certified electrician to install the proper outlets or wiring.

Maybe all you need is a small space for paying bills, reading a book and writing letters. Setting up a small side table in dining room, bedroom or kitchen, with all your supplies and stationery in a decorative box

would actually be a nice focal point in a room that is otherwise kept simple and under used, unless entertaining.

A desk for these smaller needs is the perfect fit for that space in a window alcove, under a staircase or in an entry hall. Even adding an extra-wide ledge under the windowsill would give that creative and passionate writer a space to be inspired.

Determine how long you actually use the office space. Most families only spend a few hours of the day at their desk. Using a corner of the kitchen counter or buffet table may be enough space for a laptop and a small file holder. If you have a home-based business, you may need a bit more room and a bit more privacy.

Generally, home offices that are in the bedroom or family room become a catchall type of space. It is very hard to ignore an unmade bed, piles of laundry and a sink full of dirty dishes when you have work to get done. It is too easy to just set down the mail, kid's schoolwork and other cluttering items on the desk assuming you will sort it all later. Your desk space should always remain clear and ready for use. Keeping your office area away from the family living area you are more likely to get things accomplished when you sit down. Neither the children nor the television will be disruptive as you are focusing on

work. However, this may cause you to create more to-do piles in other rooms. If the bedroom were the only place for your office, a stylish cabinet desk would make a nice choice. Having the ability to close your desk space when you are not using it keeps the bedroom atmosphere a bit more serene.

Keep a counter-top organizer or a secondary workspace in the location you perform the smaller tasks. In it place stationery, desk supplies, stamps and note pads. These counter top organizers are also available with file folder compartments and other features.

A bill payer's desk, on wheels, allows you to move your workspace to where you need it, without creating another office zone.

The bedroom, as we have already established, is your retreat space. By establishing it as your home office too, you may have a clash of interests. Keep your bedroom office-free and you could possibly be more productive. When you sit at your desk with work to be done, but constantly glance at the bed, you may start to feel sleepy. In turn, when you lay in bed to rest and you have that pile of work on the desk in your vision, it may be difficult to rest peacefully. If the bedroom is the only option for you, try to create a space that can be closed off with a freestanding screen that can hide the office when it is not in use. Choosing matching or coordinating furniture and accessories for your office that compliment your existing bedroom will reduce the feel of having the office in your bedroom. You still want your bedroom to be inviting, so it is imperative to keep organized.

 Allow plenty of time for your Home Office makeover, wherever it is in your home. Begin the project with the **'Ten Minute Tidy'**. It is usual for ten minutes to not be enough time to get through the whole office area. Working in smaller portions for this room may be necessary. It takes extra time to review documents for account information and important dates. Once you have worked through everything in ten minute increments, begin the **'3-Box-Method'** to eliminate clutter from your workspace.

You will need a few additional supplies handy in order to sort through this area successfully. Before you begin, you should gather or purchase some proper office paper management items.

These items include:
- ❖ Manila file folders
- ❖ Post-it® notes, for temporary labeling
- ❖ Hanging Pendaflex® folders
- ❖ Pencil or pen
- ❖ Plastic labels for hanging files
- ❖ Extra trash bags
- ❖ Cardboard file box or bin for temporary sorting

Use the follow list to sort your items into the **Keep, Sell/Donate** or **Discard** boxes or bags in the '**3-Box-Method**' of organizing:

✓ Up-to-date computer parts ✓ Clean printer paper ✓ Fresh ink ✓ Sufficient lighting ✓ Desk supplies in good condition ✓ Note cards and stationery ✓ Business supplies from current job ✓ Extra pens, staples, clips, envelopes, calculator and stamps ✓ Current files and statements	✓ Technologically up-to-date software and computer parts ✓ Duplicate accessories you never use ✓ Video games you no longer play ✓ Books and manuals for current interests ✓ Software programs you have copied to your hard drive	✓ Broken or out-dated computer parts and software ✓ Business cards and letterhead from past employment ✓ Pens that don't write ✓ Scissors that don't cut ✓ Printers that don't print ✓ Floppy disks you no longer reference ✓ Documents over 7 years old no longer needed for Federal Tax Returns(see additional list)

A fabric drape or a beaded door curtain can also be hung from the ceiling, installing a rod from wall to wall, diagonally so that a corner of the room is sectioned off. This curtain can be drawn closed while you are not working or do not want to see your work and opened when you are using your computer or desk surface. This too would allow ample light to enter your office space while you are working.

If you can spare some storage space, a large closet can also double as an office. It is a rather ideal set-up. Shelving can hold your supplies and it would be easy to keep that zone organized. If the office can be well maintained and decorated nicely, try removing the closet door, opening your office into view. By allowing it to be seen as an extension of another room, your space will appear larger and well designed. You will allow in more of the natural light and it can enlarge the look the adjoining room. No matter where your office space winds up, the function of this space remains the same.

Whether you already have existing office furniture or you are in need of new, the most important thing when choosing or using office furniture is to have everything very handy and easily accessible. The more times you have to get up from your work to find supplies and files, the less productive you will be and the more time that will be wasted.

A desk should be large enough to allow the use of your home computer as well as a flat surface for working. By not having a large enough surface area to accommodate the type of work you do, the there is a tendency to start piling papers on the floor around you or sticking them into drawers, leading to a space that is unmanageable.

A file credenza is a nice way to disguise your office paperwork. Appearing to be a bookcase, a credenza can hold several household files as well as having shelving for your decorative accents or additional storage containers.

A suitable desk should have several drawers that vary in depth. A number of shallow drawers to hold office supplies (pens,  stapler, index cards, etc.) and some a bit deeper for other needs (disks, CDs, envelopes). If the drawers are too deep, small items can get lost. Use small open containers or a drawer divider to keep everything in its place. It should also have a file drawer in which you keep your current statements, projects or assignments.

❖ Shelving can hold the bulky desk items like software CDs and extra desk supplies. A binder style album is ideal for music CDs and software or computer game disks. By eliminating all of the plastic jewel cases and boxes, there will be more space for other things.

❖ Keep your files, accounts or individual family member's work separated by purchasing hanging file holders and folders in different colors. Designating one color for each person or task will make locating work easier. You can also designate a separate file folder color for different interests. For example, you can keep your finance documents in green folders to represent items dealing with money. Your military documents can be kept in red folders, and so on.

❖ A good desk chair is one of the best investments you can make when designing your home office space. Choose a chair that is adjustable and has good lumbar support for your lower back. A chair that is too low or too high can cause back discomfort, or put you at an awkward height to work well.

A chair with large arms can prevent you from sitting close enough to the desk or moving about your workspace if you need to get up and down often. Smaller spaces may only allow for a basic rolling style desk chair. There are still options for good support without the bells and whistles. You will be spending a lot of time seated in your chair, make sure it is comfortable.

If you overload your file drawer with out-of-date and completed paperwork, keeping on top of your current issues will be difficult. Paperwork can be overwhelming and can accumulate when we are not looking. Controlling the paper in our lives deserves constant attention and a system all its own. Check with your financial institution regarding storing paperwork for your tax records. The 7-year rule applies to documents that you have submitted for your Federal Tax Returns. Other documents such as monthly telephone bills and bank statements do not fall under this rule. Further along in this section, a more itemized list of paper keeps and paper tosses will be listed.

Becoming emotionally tied to paper is one of the biggest problems that people, especially parents, have when it comes to the home office. Think how often you stash away birthday and thank you cards, children's artwork and recipes? Do we ever really get more pleasure from these things beyond the initial moment we receive them? Then why do we hold onto them so dearly? What purpose can they serve by keeping them? Some feel military families need to keep their home inventory minimized, so it is important to hold on to the things we treasure most. Relocating does not allow an over accumulation of storage or household items and prevents unused bits and pieces from being tucked away never to be seen again. But why leave all those paper memories for the next generation to deal with? Training yourself to instill the memory in your mind and then let go of the nonsense will drastically reduce the amount of paper that takes over and disrupts our lives.

Try this effortless method to controlling the paper things we think we need and love so much. Provide every family member with a storage box. This box should be no larger than 12" x 16" and 10" deep. In this box, only, can you keep things not quite ready to be parted with. Whether it be school papers, artwork or greeting cards, when this box gets full, it must be sorted through and purged down to make room for new memories. Let each family member be responsible for his or her own box. Suggest that it is kept in their bedroom closet or designate an accessible area of your  storage space. This will eliminate the blame if something gets lost or gets thrown out before its time.

After a while, the importance and sentimentality of these items decreases and that treasure will become a thing of the past and will be easier to eliminate. You eliminate clutter...you eliminate stress.

Use a separate storage system or file cabinet for archive paperwork (tax returns, LESs, Orders, Claims) household manuals, etc. This storage system should be kept in a closet or a basement, not in your presently operating office. Keep past files clearly labeled and neatly bundled together, so when it comes time for you to discard them, after the seven year rule, there is no need to sort through years of files.

A corner on top of the desk should hold a few shallow or wire baskets or a  paper sorter for immediate needs or items that are time sensitive. Label these baskets or pockets READ, ACT and FILE, otherwise known as the RAF System, according to professional organizers. Make it a point to keep the amount of paper in these baskets at a minimum. Either weekly or monthly, set aside a few minutes to complete the tasks in each basket. By doing this often, it will not become a major project.

All other needs for the office can be placed on shelves above the desk, or on a bookcase within reaching distance to the workspace. Using additional baskets or decorative boxes, clearly labeled with its contents, your office space will look neat and you will feel more productive. The main idea is for everything to have its own place. When you take something out, put it back where it belongs when you are finished. The next time you need it, you'll know where to find it.

Before you run out and purchase office furniture, you may want to have a look around your house. You may have something that can be transformed from its original purpose to create the perfect (or at least perfect for that duty station) desk or shelf.

❖ Two identical height filing cabinets or nightstands make great support for a thick piece of wood or an old flat door. With a coat of fresh paint or wallpaper, your surface will appear as though you had custom work done.

❖ Look at garage sales or furniture salvage stores for interesting flat surfaces. Old marble slabs, coffee table tops and even stained glass windows can make for extraordinary workspaces. If the surface you choose is a bit uneven, have a piece of glass, or plexi-glass, cut to cover it. Be sure to have the edges beveled to prevent accidental injuries. This way you can enjoy the details of your unique find, without having to cover it up. An antique dressing table, a small hall or sofa table cannot only be functional but also very decorative.

In addition to the traditional metal filing cabinets, there are many other varieties on the market that do not appear so institutional. The sturdiest of them all, even over the metal ones, are made from solid wood. You can get them in a number of finishes or colors and they usually have a bit of trim work on them to dress them up. Depending on the number of people needing to store files in them, they also come in heights up to four drawers high. They can  accent a room as another piece of furniture or a small wall unit.

Files can also be stored in deep baskets, old wine crates or steamer trunks. Almost anything can be transformed to hold the hanging file folders as long as you have the wire frame to support the weight. If the frame fits into your storage, so will the files.

You can have a very special office space to call your own, and it is ok to have beautiful furniture and unique accents, just keep your finds functional. When too many "things" start accumulating on the top of the desk and the floor around it, you will infringe on that clean and productive area with clutter again.

Above all, your workspace should inspire you and motivate you to be productive and successful. It should allow you to relax and stay focused on the task at hand.

Power Paper Purge List:

The following paper items can be sorted through and discarded on a regular basis. It is recommended you check with your financial institution for a more detailed list of archiving documents for Federal Tax Returns. This list refers to the typical household situation.

- ✓ Expired coupons
- ✓ Resumes: Once you have updated your resume, discard old versions, keeping only the current copy.
- ✓ Correspondence: Old note cards, invitations and memos
- ✓ Product User Guides and Manuals: Once you have learned the operation or the warranty is no longer honored
- ✓ Household Inventory: Keep most current copy
- ✓ Credit Card Statements: Keep statements for tax purposes, once you receive the End of Year (EOY) Statement, you can discard individual monthly statements.
- ✓ Bank Statements: Keep for 6 years plus present year
- ✓ Canceled Checks: only keep for tax purposes until EOY Statement
- ✓ ATM Receipts: Once they appear documented on your monthly statement, you can discard the slips
- ✓ Military Orders: Keep one original copy of each document. Once you reach your new assignment, duplicates of past assignment orders are no longer needed

Designate one storage bin for archived tax paperwork. After filing your return, gather all documents and secure together in an envelope or with a rubber band and clearly mark with the date. This creates a rotating paper cycle. Each year when adding the current documents to the bin, remove the earliest dated documents and dispose of them properly, preferably using a shredder. The bin should hold 7 years of Federal Tax Return documents.

<u>Notes</u>

The Home Office: Floor Planning Template

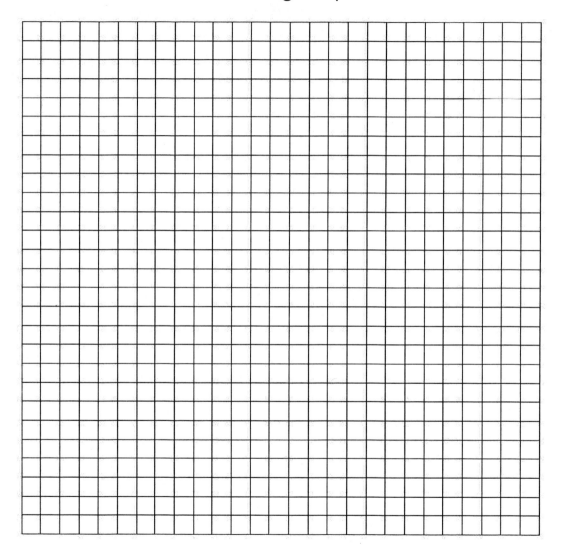

You CAN Do-It-Yourself

With this fast paced industry of remodeling and redecorating homes, the public resources available for homeowners to take on do-it-yourself projects are at their peak. Television shows and even networks are dedicating themselves entirely to teaching eager novices the tricks of the trade in home interior and exterior decorating. There are a few things they will never tell you, but I will.

First of all, the time it normally takes to clear a room completely, clean out years worth of clutter, have a yard sale to sell it all, design, rebuild, paint, refurnish and redecorate is much longer than what they make it appear to be. Secondly, they forget to mention the rest of the twenty or more crewmembers and subcontractors that were also used to finish the job in two days. They do not mention that the lead-time for ordering new furniture and fabrics can be at a minimum of 4 weeks, and another 2 weeks to do all the sewing and upholstering. Thirdly, the majority of the wood they use to custom make cabinetry and built-ins is made from Medium Density Fiberboard, MDF or manufactured particleboard and would never last through multiple moves. Refer to 'Making Smart Purchases for Your Home' for a more detailed explanation of MDF.

To make a long story short, there is a lot of time and money involved in the process of completely redecorating a room. The intention of the last section of That Military House: Move it, Organize it & Decorate it, is to provide you with tips, tools, shortcuts and knowledge so you can save time and money in your home decorating and organizing projects.

Any look can be re-created with patience and practice. Sometimes it takes making some mistakes to learn the ins and outs of the trade. These mistakes can be limited if you follow the steps outlined for you.

The knowledge you will learn here will allow you to:

- ❖ Paint a room with precision using tricks of the trade and money saving suggestions.
- ❖ Learn and apply a variety of hand-stitches to hem curtains, make pillows and add trims or accents to your existing linens.
- ❖ Operate your sewing machine and sew in a straight line.
- ❖ Hang a group of pictures on the wall and have them look perfect the first time.
- ❖ Make your long curtains shorter and your short curtains longer.
- ❖ Use what you have to add a unique touch to your home.

PAINTING A ROOM:

When undertaking a painting project, it is important that you have the proper tools. By using tools that are not designed for the task, your final outcome will not be clean and professional looking. Using brushes that are too wiry or rollers that are too thin will make your painting experience more of a hassle than a pleasure. Stay away from fancy rolling edging contraptions and other invented gadgets. They take a lot of practice to master and are rather costly.

Before you head out the door, be sure that you have taken rough measurements of the room. Having these dimensions will ensure that you don't under-buy or over-buy a quantity of paint. Sales associates at the paint counter are sometimes not very knowledgeable when it comes to answering questions involving the details of your project. If you feel that you need an employee with more experience, don't hesitate to ask for someone else's opinion.

For the measurement process of painting a room, it is not necessary to figure out the dimensions down to the ½ inch. A rough estimate will do just as well.

Consider the windows and doorways as part of the wall. This will give you a little extra paint for edging and touch-ups. Using  a measuring tape is the easiest and recommended way to determine the square footage of a room, but just walking it out is ok too. Measure the room one wall at a time. You can safely assume that your ceiling height is 8', unless you know differently.

Tools needed:

- Paint tray
- Tall Kitchen trash bags
- A small, disposable bowl or container
- Paint roller; one that the nap is not too flat but not too thick. The packaging on the roller will recommend the 'nap' required for specific paint types (i.e. flat or semi-gloss)

- Paint roller handle, double check that your roller fits the handle
- Paint stirrer (free with the purchase of paint)
- Paint can opener or can key (to avoid making dents in the lip of the can)
- Low-tack masking tape or blue painter's tape to tape off tricky spots (a little more $ but works the best and won't peel existing paint when you remove it)

- A large, thick rubber band that will fit around the paint can height wise
- 2 Paint brushes; one that is soft, 1 ½ inches wide and has a beveled edge for accurate edging and another that is firm and about 3 inches wide

- A damp sponge or cloth; to wipe up drips
- Ladder or step stool; high enough that you will not have to reach for spots

- Screwdriver; to remove the outlet covers and lighting fixtures.
- Drop cloth; to cover any furniture you think you may get too close to
- Spackling compound and sand paper if you are filling holes

Don't get confused between the square footage of a room and the square footage of the wall space. This can result in a major paint quantity error. At a minimum, know that typically, one gallon of paint will cover approximately a 9'x12' room once. If you want to paint two coats, that's two gallons of paint. However, if you have the time for a quick room measurement, it is very advisable:

❖ Place the tape along the baseboard of the first wall.
❖ Write down the measurement to the closest foot, round up rather than down.
❖ Measure the wall from ceiling to floor, use the corner of the room for the most accurate reading, or assume 8' standard ceiling height.
❖ Write down that measurement. Round up to the nearest foot.
❖ Multiply the two numbers together to get the square footage of that wall.
❖ Do all the walls in the same method.
❖ Add all your square foot measurements together.
❖ You now have the square footage of the wall space.

Here is where Do-It-Yourself projects can get tricky. In order to save money on supply costs, you have to do your homework and know exactly what it is you need. Otherwise you can be taken by those sales pitches and marketing strategies. If you know you want the less expensive household brand versus a signature designer brand, make that clear. By familiarizing yourself with paint vocabulary, you will know what is needed for your project and you will save money and time during the purchasing phase. Remember if you find a color you really love in a designer brand, most stores will be able to match the color and mix it using a less expensive base.

Remember your first stop on the way to pick up your supplies is the DIY store or the Self Help Store that is on your military installation. Here you can get several items needed at no charge. Safe things to take here are the paint tray, trash bags, paint stirrer and a paint roller with a handle. If there is a nice selection of brushes, you may find what you are looking for.

When you have to purchase painting tools, **do not skimp on quality brushes**. With a proper brush you can eliminate hours spent taping off the baseboards, ceiling, doorways and fixtures.

Paints are available in basically two types, water–based and oil-based. Water based paints are recommended because they are faster drying, easier to clean up and have minimal odors. They come in several finishes:

- ❖ **Flat** (good for ceilings)
- ❖ **Eggshell** (good for kitchens, bathrooms and walls with flaws)
- ❖ **Satin/semi-gloss** (nice for interior walls with medium wear and tear, holds up to cleaning; Great in kitchens, bathrooms and children's rooms)
- ❖ **Glossy** (very shiny, sometimes too shiny), use on baseboards, trim and doors

Oil-based paints take longer to dry, have toxic fumes and require potent chemicals for clean up. Not great for use around children or in small spaces. Oil-based paints are, on the other hand, very durable and long lasting. They too come in the same variety of finishes.

When you are choosing paint, consider the surface area that you are painting. If it has been previously painted, you should take extra time and apply a primer to the walls. For example, the person who lived there before you painted the walls with an interior latex paint; you purchase an acrylic paint and without priming try to paint the walls. What happens is the two different types of paint will not bond causing your paint to roll on streaky and uneven and if scratched after drying, the fresh paint will peel off like a sticker. Not good! If you are certain that the paint types are compatible, it is okay  to eliminate the priming step. Priming is recommended when you are painting a light color over a pre-existing dark color.

Step 1: Bring home paint samples.
Step 2: Tape to the wall and watch over a few days.
Step 3: Narrow down choices and buy testers.
Step 4: Buy paint to complete project.

As mentioned previously, when you are making choices about which color to paint your room, it is wise to test a small area of the wall to be sure the color you choose is the one that will look best. By painting this test patch, about a 3'x3' area, directly onto the wall you not only will be sure the color is right but you will also confirm that the type of paint you have chosen will work well when applied to the wall.

A less permanent technique to making that color decision is to paint the tester color on a 3'x3' piece of butcher paper, a piece of artist's canvas or even scrap wood. Tape it up, hang it or lean it against the wall.

Spend a day or two observing the color at different times of the day and in different lighting, natural and artificial. Move the samples onto different walls for different views. Now is the time to make changes to the color before you make an investment.

When you are certain about your choice, go ahead and purchase the appropriate number gallons of paint and begin. Painting the walls and ceilings is the most common home decorating project. By following the steps to preparing your painting area and painting the walls, your room will be finished in a snap.

Preparing your painting area is important in the timeliness of the project. Having all of your supplies within reach can make the difference between smooth walls or walls with ridges. Ridges develop when a thick area of paint is left too long to dry, before being smoothed out or blended in.

❖ Gather your tools and supplies into one corner or space in the room.
❖ Move all furniture to the middle of the room, roll up the carpet if possible, and take all of the picture hangers and nails out of the walls.
❖ Fill holes with spackling and sand until smooth. Small holes do not need to be filled. The paint will be enough to fill it as you roll.

❖ Cover your furniture with a drop cloth. Wall-to-wall carpeting can be covered with an additional drop cloth while you are painting an area and moved along as you progress around the room.

❖ Lie out an open trash bag and keep all paint materials on it at all times.

❖ Open the can of paint and mix thoroughly, very thoroughly. *If using more than one can of paint of the same color, get a large bucket and combine both cans together to ensure a perfect, even color throughout the room.

❖ Very carefully stretch the rubber band over the opening of the can and under the bottom, use this to remove excess paint from your brush instead of the side of the can.

❖ Open your brushes and flick through the bristles to remove dust and any loose bristles that may wind up on the walls, dried into the paint later.

❖ Place the paint tray inside a trash bag and secure with masking tape. When it's time for clean up just invert the bag and toss, leaving the tray completely dry and clean.

❖ Open the rollers and cover with masking tape, peel off the tape to remove loose fibers so they don't end up on your walls. The better the quality of roller you buy the less fiber there will be to remove.

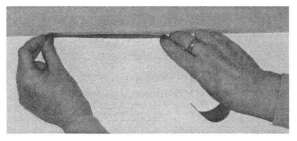

Cover or tape around anything that can't be removed, like the thermostat, outlets or light fixtures. Wipe down the area to be painted with a damp sponge since dust on the walls can create small bubbles and bumps in the fresh paint. Take the time to prepare the room correctly and your painting project will go much smoother and produce a more professional look.

Masking tape can also be used around every ceiling edge and baseboard. This process takes a little extra time, but doing so can leave you with very accurate edges. Be sure to peel off the tape as soon as you are finished painting. Allowing too long of the drying time to pass may result in uneven edges as you peel off the tape.

Begin "cutting-in" or painting a stripe around your ceiling edges, baseboards and any other areas that will not be reached by a roller. Start in a top corner of the room and use the beveled edge brush. Pour a small amount of paint into a disposable bowl to use while you are on a ladder or step stool. Carrying a full can of paint up and down ladder steps or on and off a chair or stool can result in a very large and messy spill, one that can only be horrifying when it happens.

"Cutting-in" an edge while painting:

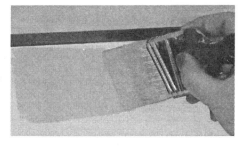

❖ When painting an edge near the ceiling, angle your hand so that the brush's beveled edge moves straight across the wall, parallel to the ceiling, and about ¼" to ½" away from the ceiling itself. If the previous paint color will show in this small space, you will then have to carefully get as close to the edge as possible.

❖ Apply enough pressure to the brush so the bristles start to flex. Do not try to

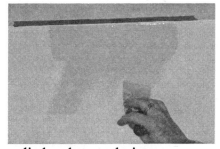

get the brush all the way into the actual edge, you will run the chance of getting paint on the ceiling. This could result in having to touch up or repaint the ceiling.

❖ Keeping away from the ceiling a bit will also makes the ceiling appear higher. It allows for clean edges and touch-ups. Use less paint than you think. It is always easier to add more than take it off once it is applied and starts drying.

- ❖ Once a small section of the edge is painted straight, drag the paint down from the edge to smooth out any ridges.
- ❖ Paint down about 4" from the edges while you are there on the ladder. This will allow you a little leeway when you begin rolling. There will be no need to roll too close to the edging and therefore no accidental bumps with the roller on the ceiling.
- ❖ Continue the same technique along the baseboards, floor, doorways and fixtures. Leave the same ¼" to ½" space. Use ½" to ¼" tape if you need to and tape directly on the wall to be painted. This may save you time and reduce the amount of accidents.

Once the entire room is "cut in", then you can begin to "roll-out" the rest of the room with your paint roller.

"Rolling-out" while painting:

- ❖ Pour paint into the tray almost up to the top of the reservoir.
- ❖ Dip the roller into the paint and roll it along the grooved section of the tray so that the roller fills with paint. The roller should be covered but not dripping with paint when you take it away from the tray.
- ❖ Begin rolling an upward stroke then a diagonal stroke down to the right across the wall to prevent dripping.
- ❖ Move the roller slowly, applying slight pressure. Moving the roller too fast can cause spattering of the paint that may end up on the floor or you furniture.
- ❖ Bring the roller upward and into the opposite diagonal and back down. You are sort of making the letter "M" on the wall.(Work in 3' x 3' increments)

❖ Continue to fill in the "M" area until the paint is smooth and there are no visible strokes.

❖ Once the section is evenly filled in, move the roller one last time vertically over the area, repeat this over each area to form continuity between sections and to polish the final look of the walls.

Concentrate on one small section at a time; do not try to cover a large amount of space with one load of the roller. If you use the proper techniques, you will save yourself the time of having to touch up or apply a whole second coat. Depending on the color you have chosen and the color you are covering over, a second coat still may be necessary. Good technique will result in beautiful walls.

Remember when you are choosing your color; if the color on the sample is what you want the room to look like, you may want to choose a color that is a shade or two lighter than the one you desired. The room color will appear several shades darker once you cover a large space.

Painting projects often take time and always require sufficient drying time between coats, usually a few hours. Cleaning up your supplies, just to get it all out again tomorrow can take at the minimum one hour. So, once your first coat is finished, empty the paint still left in the tray back into the can. Place the roller, still wet and loaded with paint, into a clean, plastic bag, close it up and tie it shut with a twist- tie or tape. If you are waiting over night before painting again put it in the refrigerator. Yes, the refrigerator! When you are ready to paint the next day, just thaw out the roller and off you go. Same rule applies to the paintbrush. Invert the plastic bag that was housing the paint tray and toss. Clean up is finished.

SEWING BASICS

You may decide to take on a decorating project that involves a bit of sewing. Whether it is hemming draperies, making new throw pillows or designing new curtains, hiring a seamstress to do the job for you can end up costing you a lot of money by the time the work is finished. There are several alternative methods available to those who want to make things themselves but don't have the coordination it takes to make them. Some stores carry products that can actually assist you in your endeavors without you ever having to sewing a stitch.

Most of us own a sewing machine for one reason or another, but knowing how to operate it is a different story. The sewing machine you own may have been a wedding gift from your mother or a hand me down from a friend or neighbor, it may have an instruction manual or not. You can contact the manufacturer and request a copy of the manual or download it from the manufacturer's website. One thing is for certain; most sewing machines basically operate with the same steps and can produce the same beautiful home décor accents whether they are the $99 model or the $1000+ professional model.

Putting all the fancy work aside that may seem daunting and complicated, and mastering the basic techniques to a perfect straight-line stitch, sewing on a button and hand stitching for repairs, you can save time and money by doing the work yourself.

If you are up for the challenge but do not own a sewing machine, you may want to think about investing in one. Look at second hand shops and mass-market

stores. Stores that specialize in sewing supplies are usually a bit pricier and come with a salesperson that will focus on showing off the fancy features and may convince you to spend more money than you intended. To start off your new hobby, purchase a machine that has a few basic stitch options and that the feet required for zippers and buttonholes are included. Beyond that, you may be paying for features you will never even utilize. In the future, if you decide to further your talents, you can always upgrade.

Undoubtedly, you will find that every house you're making a home will have different window sizes, shapes, closure types and frameworks. Buying new curtains each time you relocate would be a major expense. To lessen the need for purchasing new window treatments for each place, it's best to create curtains that will be suitable for a variety of situations.

Windows can be dressed very simply or quite elaborately depending on your skill and budget. Curtains enhance a nice window and can also disguise faults in an unattractive one. They provide privacy or obscure a bad view. If you are lucky enough to have a beautiful view, you may want to consider a simple swag either alone or over a sheer panel.

If you're just getting started, here are some helpful hints to assure that your sewing endeavors are a success. It is good practice to 'measure twice, cut once'. When measuring the length and width for your window dressing, take into consideration, which type of curtain rod you plan to use and where it will hang.

✧ Tension rods sit tightly inside the frame of the window.

✧ Single Bracket Rods are either attached on wide window framework or on the wall a few inches beyond the frame.

✧ Double bracket rods can hold two curtain rods on the same window. They allow one window to have two layers of curtains. Perhaps sheer panels behind more decorative panels.

✧ Hidden hardware rods are ideal for window treatments where the hardware is not part of the design. This type of rod is good for attaching to the ceiling when hanging a dividing curtain or bed canopy.

 ✧ Thin iron or metal rods are a recommended choice for small valances or café curtains, also ideal for smaller windows in bathrooms and entry areas. Iron rods can be dressed up a bit by adding ornate finials and are available in several varieties.

 ✧ Wooden curtain rods add character and weight to a window treatment. Made of unfinished wood, they can be painted or stained to match any room's décor. Screw-on finials allow for an affordable change.

 ✧ Rod finials can be purchased in combination with matching rods or separately. Ranging from flowers to soccer balls, there are finials out there for every room. Coordinating tie-backs can also be purchased for added detail.

After choosing and hanging the rod, measure the window width at the outside of the framework and the length from the top of the rod to the lowest point where you want your curtains to end. Determine whether you want the curtains to hang to the windowsill, to the floor, or somewhere in between. For a valance or café curtain, the same instructions will apply.

Fabrics are available in a variety of widths from 36" to 60" wide. Traditionally, a curtain width measures one and a half to two times the width of the window. This allows for gathering of the fabric on the rod. When determining the yardage of fabric for the length, remember to allow for a rod pocket, a hem and the total length of the finished curtain. Reminder: curtains that hang longer will better adapt to another location down the line. Double this length you measured, assuming you want two curtain panels, one for each side of the window. Generally, 6 ½" is allowed for a rod pocket and 3 ½" for the hem. The same measuring techniques apply whether you are machine or hand sewing.

No-Sew Drapery:

By purchasing a large cut of yardage for a window you allow yourself the opportunity to create an almost unlimited amount of custom "looking" window treatments. By gathering and draping the fabric, you will be able to manipulate the fabric yardage into beautiful rosettes, bishop sleeves and swags. The following curtain styles and their instructional methods are my personal favorite recommendations:

❖ Rubber Band Rosettes: Drape your fabric over the ends of the curtain rods at the approximate length you need for the curtain to reach the floor or windowsill. Grab the needed amount fabric into one hand that will bring the curtain to the desired length. Pull the fabric through the rubber band, like you are pulling hair through for a ponytail. Double over the rubber band until tight. Spread the bundled fabric out into the shape of a rosette. Hook or hang the rubber band onto the rod hardware to secure the rosette. Repeat to the other corner.

❖ Bishop's Sleeve: Curtain panels that are too long can be easily lifted off the floor by adding a Bishop's Sleeve. Determine the height on the window frame you would like the tieback treatment to hang. At that point, screw a cup hook or hammer a small nail into the side of the window frame. Using string, dental floss or ribbon. Gather the panel and tie the string around it at a point about 8-10 inches lower than the hook. Lift the string onto the hook and fluff out the draping fabric into the look of a shirtsleeve.

❖ Accented Bishop's Sleeve: The style of the Bishop's Sleeve is beautiful in itself, but it also opens its beauty to details and accents through embellishments that you can find throughout your house. Tassels, scarves and jewelry add a unique touch to this tie back treatment.

❖ Slip Knot: Fabric yardage can be attached to a curtain rod using a slipknot. Drape one end of the fabric up and over the rod, about two to three feet. Take the shorter length of fabric from the back and wrap it around the longer length of fabric in the front. Continue wrapping until the end of the fabric begins to come around the front again. Tuck the tail of the short end into the initial fabric wrap. The front of the window treatment will look like a knot in a man's tie. This treatment can be repeated to both sides of the window. The bottom raw edge of the fabric, closest to the floor, can be left to "puddle". Tuck the unfinished edge under and into itself. Leave some fabric length and blouse out the bottom of the curtain.

❖ Fabric Loops: Fabric yardage can also be hung over a curtain rod using repetitive loops up and over the rod. Be sure to hide the raw edges within the gathers. Any number of loops can be made in order to create the desired look or the desired length.

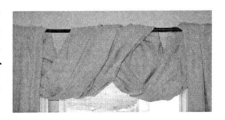

❖ Use a variety of the previous methods at the same time to adjust extra long yardage or to change the look of the window treatment. Without sewing or fancy hardware, you can have amazing window treatments that look custom designed by an interior decorator.

There are many other household types of linen that can be converted into valance or café dressings for your windows. Look through your wardrobe accessories, closets and kitchen drawers. There are more items than you may think that can be used non-traditionally to suit your temporary needs for your windows. The answer here is to use items without having to sew in rod pockets, buy new curtains every time you relocate or to have curtains custom made to fit each window's needs.

Whether there are curtain rods already installed, you have your own from previous homes or you need to purchase rods, there are ways of utilizing linens without sewing a stitch.

Curtain rings with spring clips can be easily attached to fabric and slid onto a rod. There are fabric clips that can be used to bunch and gather yardage into creative shapes and styles. Use large binder clips in the office, hair "claw" clips for a girl's room and neckties in a boy's room.

❖ Cloth Napkins are perfect to use for your kitchen windows. Choose napkins that coordinate with your dishes, so they can be used again at a new location. Attach curtain rings with clips evenly spaced apart and slide them onto a tension rod.

❖ Cloth napkins can also be used to create a decorative valance on an additional window treatment in the same room or in an eat-in-kitchen area. Great idea

too for a bathroom. Fold the cloth napkins in half diagonally, tuck in the edges and press with a hot iron. Drape the napkins over the curtain rod and shift them as needed to cover the length of the rod. You can leave the points out or fold them under, depending on the look you want.

❖ New or Vintage table linens make fun curtain valances. Using a table linen as a valance can be an interesting way to add charm to a room. There are tables linens for every holiday and can be easily changed, as can the cloth napkins, throughout the seasons. Fold the linen over the rod and use ribbon, straw raffia, scarves or neckties to complete the look.

❖ A pashmina scarf or shoulder wrap makes an elegant addition to any window. Most appealing draped over the rod, backed by a sheer curtain panel.

It is possible to make curtains even if you don't own a sewing machine, and without even hand-sewing a stitch. If you've never heard of fusible webbing, or Stitch Witchery™, let me introduce you to this fabulous product. Fusible webbing is a fabric interfacing used to prevent fabric from unraveling. This product is sold in a variety of widths in yardage or as a spool in blister packages. Applied with an iron, the webbing has a bonding agent (resembling a 'web' of glue) activated by heat. It can be purchased at a fabric store or in the sewing and craft section of your local five and dime or super store.

No-Sew Fusible Webbing:

❖ When using fusible webbing: fold and press all areas that would normally be sewn. For instance, press the raw edge of the hem into a folded position as though it was being hemmed.

❖ Open the fold and cut a strip of fusible webbing the length of the area.

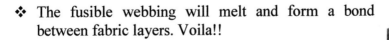

❖ Lay the webbing between the layers of fabric you want adhered together and press down the seam with a hot iron. Flip over the fabric and press again. If the fabric allows, use a little steam. Moisture will transfer the heat through the fabric better.

❖ The fusible webbing will melt and form a bond between fabric layers. Voila!!

❖ Repeat this process on all areas that would be 'sewn'.

*By the way, this product can be used on any fabric or garment requiring a no-sew hem.

As a reminder, it doesn't have to cost a fortune to decorate your home. Linen towels, cloth napkins as well as soft placemats placed strategically over a rod at the kitchen window make a clever valance. They can be changed with the seasons if you choose. Think about using items for other than what they were intended. Use scarves, tablecloths, and even pillowcases to add a unique touch. Don't be afraid to try things out. You can always take them down if you are not pleased with the result. Experimentation is the key to expanding your creative mind.

For the aspiring seamstress out there, you can ease your way into the world of sewing by first experimenting with a few basic hand-sewing stitches. With these stitches you will be able to create window treatments, accent pillows and covers and attach stylish trims to already existing items in your home. The most basic of sewn window treatments is the swag, in which you can finish off the selvage edges of your yardage with a clean hem.

Low–Sew Swag:

Lengths of fabric alone can be used to create elegantly draped window treatments, like the ones shown previously in the No-Sew examples. The difference is that you will be hemming the raw and selvage edges of the yardage. This requires a minimal amount of sewing. Here's how:

- ❖ Determine the amount of fabric you'll need by simply using a piece of rope or string.
- ❖ Hang the rope over the already hung rod, letting it lay loosely up, over, and around the rod and then down, as you would like the fabric to fall in place.
- ❖ Before you cut the rope at the point where you've decided the length is to end, add maybe 4" more on each side for hems or adjustments.
- ❖ Now, take the rope off of the rod and measure its length.

This is the amount of yardage you would purchase to create your swag. The extra inches will also assure the window treatment will adapt to a new window in your next house. No need to re-buy curtains.

The only parts of the fabric swag that you may want to finish are the ends of the yardage, the ends that were cut at the fabric store. If not, you can tie each end into a large knot, and hide the raw edges of the fabric. If you would rather finish the edge, without a sewing machine, you would hand stitch using a 'running stitch'. This is a simple stitch made by running the thread over and under the fabric.

Running Stitch:

❖ Measure and fold the fabric 1" from the edge, iron this crease.

❖ Fold ½ of that previous fold into itself and iron that crease. What you have now is a rolled, flat hem that needs stitching, by hand or by machine.

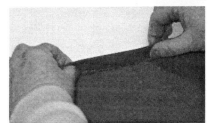

❖ By hand, thread the needle, knot off the long end and push the needle down through the fabric pulling it all the way through to the knot.

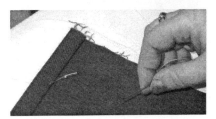

❖ Push the needle back up a 1/16" away from where you first went through. Repeat.

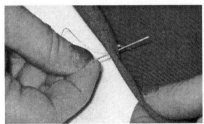

❖ Continue the stitch until you come to the end of your fabric. The stitch is literally weaving in and out, in even increments, along the hem about 1/16" from the fold.

❖ To end the stitch, do 3 stitches on top of each other. This is stronger than a knot. Unless the selvage (raw manufactured sides of your fabric) contains printed words, it can be left unfinished. Even if there is printing on the selvage, the edges can be tucked under so the printing is not revealed.

Remember, hand sewing is an option if you don't have access to a machine. When you are going to sew by hand, choose a needle suitable for the fabric type. 'Sharps' are used for hand sewing. The needle packaging will indicate the weight that is appropriate for the type of fabric you've chosen. Purchase 'general purpose' thread the same color or as close as possible to the fabric.

Threading a Needle:

❖ Thread a needle by cutting a piece of thread about 18-24" long. Any longer and it tends to get unruly or tangled.
❖ (Hint: If you moisten the thread with your tongue, it will pass through the needle easier.)
❖ Pull the thread through until one end is longer than the other.
❖ Knot the longer end.

Colorful accent pillows really enhance a room's décor and create a comfortable and cozy feeling in any room. However, they can be rather expensive to buy. You can either purchase fabric or recycle what you already have to make creative and eye-catching pillows. A vintage linen, a chenille spread, a favorite sweater or t-shirt someone has grown out of...they all make wonderful pillows.

Creating your own pillow only involves a few steps. If you plan to insert a pillow form, rather than a polyester filling, into the finished product, measure and cut your fabric the size of the form allowing for an additional ½" for the seam. Pin the front to the back with right sides of the fabric facing together and the edges even.

Back Stitch:

You can use a sewing machine or hand stitch the pillow using a 'back stitch'. A back stitch is a series of stitches that each overlaps half of the previous stitch. This makes a very strong seam.

❖ Thread your needle, as previously explained.
❖ Pick up a 1/8" stitch. Leave a ½" seam. This will ensure the pillow edges do not come apart once the pillow has been filled and stitched closed.

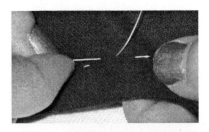

- ❖ Insert the needle 1/16" behind the initial stitch, moving halfway backwards.
- ❖ Take another 1/8" stitch, and again move back 1/16".
- ❖ Repeat this process. On one side of the fabric you will see stitches spaced 1/16" apart. On the other side of the fabric, you will see the full stitches, overlapping one another.

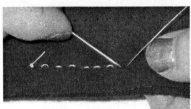

- ❖ Sew allowing the half-inch seam around 3 sides, as well as the corners of the fourth side.
- ❖ Leaving the center of the fourth side un-sewn will provide an opening to turn the pillow right side out.
- ❖ Cut away the point of fabric across the corners of the seam allowance before turning. *This will eliminate bulk in the corners of the finished pillow.

- ❖ Turn the pillow to the right side and insert the form or fiberfill stuffing.
- ❖ Turns the open edges ½" towards the inside and use a 'drawing stitch' to close the pillow.

Drawing Stitch:

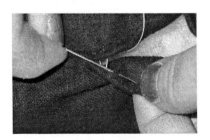

- ❖ The drawing stitch creates an invisible seam when finished. With the seams folded in, take a short stitch on one folded edge.

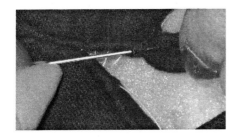

❖ Then take a short stitch on the other folded edge. Do not pull the thread taut yet. You need the opening to remain accessible to maneuver the needle. Continue this stitch across the pillow opening.

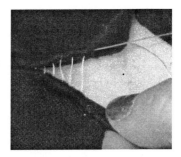

❖ The thread will be zigzagging between both inside folds of the opening.

❖ After you complete several stitches, gently pull the thread and the stitches will be drawn closed. Repeat this process until you reach the end of the opening. Back stitch a few stitches to secure the closure.

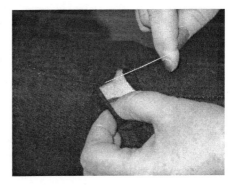

You can embellish pillows, curtains, bedding and more, by stitching tassels on the corners or beaded trims around the edges using a 'whip stitch'.

Whip Stitch:

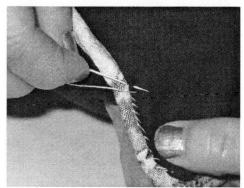

- ❖ The whip stitch is used for sewing fabrics together. These stitches are about 1/16" apart and only as deep as necessary to create a firm seam.
- ❖ Leave a 'tail' of thread when you start and work several stitches over it to secure and hide the thread.

Save money by repairing and altering your own clothing. Sewing on a button takes but a few minutes. Buttons can also be added to curtains and accent pillows.

Sewing on a Button:

- ❖ Choose a thread that either matches the thread color on the other buttons or matches the color of the garment.
- ❖ Cut a piece of thread about 18" long.
- ❖ Thread the needle and pull the thread through until the two ends are the same length so the thread is actually doubled. (Hint: if you moisten the thread with your tongue, it will go through the needle easier).

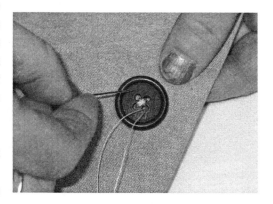

- ❖ Tie and knot the ends together.
- ❖ Hold the button in the spot you want it sewn on.
- ❖ You can place a toothpick or coin

behind the edge of the button if the fabric is thick, for example a wool coat. This prevents you from sewing the button too close to the fabric allowing space for the buttonhole side of the garment to lay behind the button when in place.

❖ Push the needle up from the back of the material and through one of the holes in the button.

❖ Now push the needle down through the next hole.

❖ Repeat this process three times, going up and down through the buttonholes and material making it secure. Knot the thread on the back of the material.

Sewing Machine Basic Operation:

Owning a sewing machine and making your own curtains and other accessories for your home can be practical, exciting and rewarding. There are many patterns available with a variety of window treatment and décor options to add beauty and comfort to your home. Get to know your sewing machine. Refer to the owner's manual and practice on some scrap fabric or an old sheet until you're comfortable. If you do not have the manual you may be able to contact the manufacturer or download the manual on-line through the manufacturer website.

Tools Needed:

- Sewing machine
- Sharp scissors (for fabric only if possible)
- Fabric / trim / and other notions
- Thread that matches the base color of your fabric
- Bobbins
- Ironing board and iron
- Straight pins
- Seam Ripper

Prepare your workspace. Allow yourself room to completely spread out the fabric that you will be working with. Set up your ironing board (very helpful to iron in your creases before you sew) and have your scissors, pins and other notions close at hand.

This section will take you through the steps to sewing a straight-line stitch. After learning this stitch, you will be able to work on your own and apply these techniques to make pillows, curtains and practically anything that requires a straight seam. Practice makes your perfect even better, so try not to get frustrated and remember, one of the wonderful things about sewing is that if a project doesn't turn out the way you want it, you can always carefully rip out the seams (with the appropriate seam ripping tool) and try again.

Pay close attention to your measurements and always double-check them before making any cuts into the fabric. Cutting is one step that cannot be reversed. For visual purposes, the steps following will demonstrate sewing a hem in a curtain panel.

Measuring and pinning your fabric
   ❖ Hang the curtain on the window and use a straight pin to mark the length you would like your finished hem to be.
   ❖ Lay your fabric out flat, on a table or clean floor.
   ❖ Use a measuring tape to establish where you placed your pin and add 2" to that measurement. Pin again.
   ❖ Fold the fabric up towards the top of the panel and stop where this new measurement is marked.
   ❖ Use the measuring tape to measure from the top of the panel to where your fabric will be cut, mark down both sides, and several places in between. Pins should be placed about 4 inches from each other.
   ❖ Cut the fabric along the line of pins.
   ❖ Remove the pins and iron the bottom edge of the fabric with a 2" fold.
   ❖ Fold this 2" into the new crease and iron in a 1" crease. You have doubled the hem.

❖ Pin the new pressed hem in a vertical angle to prevent the fabric from shifting while sewing.
❖ Re-hang the curtain to be sure the measurements will be correct.
❖ Sew the hem using the sewing machine.

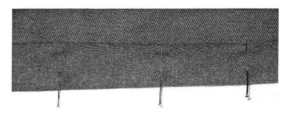

Threading the sewing machine:

Threading a sewing machine can take patience but with a little practice, you will understand the technique. Almost all machines are threaded in the same fashion, however, if your machine style is unique; you may need to refer to your User's Manual for further directions. The basic threading is completed in 6 simple steps. (Fig. A)

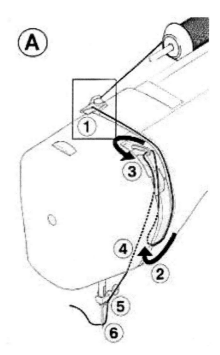

Threading a Bobbin:

Learning to thread a bobbin can be a bit more challenging and may require some practice.

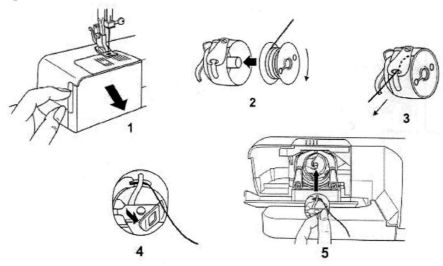

Straight Stitching using a sewing machine:

❖ Turn your stitch pattern dial to the desired stitch, usually #1 for a straight stitch.

❖ Raise the needle to its highest position and lift the foot. (Fig.1)

❖ Place the fabric under the foot, with the edge being sewn towards the inside of the machine.

❖ Move the top end fabric to line up under the needle and lower the foot. This foot will hold your fabric in place while sewing. (Fig.2)

❖ Slowly apply pressure to the foot pedal and begin sewing.

❖ One you have made the first few stitches, "backtack", or reverse the sewing to double up on the first few stitches. This backtack stitch will reinforce your seams and prevent them from coming unraveled when you clean the curtain. There is usually a reverse button for this, located on the front of the machine.

❖ Begin sewing again in the forward direction. Hold the fabric firmly to keep it from sliding out from under the foot, but not too firm because the machine will automatically pull the fabric under the foot as it sews.

❖ When you reach the end of the hem, again "backtack" the last few stitches.

❖ With the needle in the 'up' position, lift the foot, remove the fabric and cut the threads.

HANGING PICTURES ON A WALL

Hanging a grouping of pictures on a wall can be one of the most frustrating projects when it comes to the final touches of decorating a room. No matter how many times you measure, marks you make on the wall or hammer in that nail, one picture always manages to be out of line, crooked or in the wrong spot.

When hanging frames on a wall, whether it is one large print, many small pictures or a number of varying size frames there are a few good decorating tips to follow:

- Pictures of any type should be hung with their center point just slightly above the average eye-level. If there is more than one picture or it is a part of a collage, again, the center point of the group should be at the same eye level. Reason being; photos that are hung on the walls in a room become the focal point or grounding point to that space. They are hung in places that will be seen by everyone: family, friends, and neighbors. If a picture hangs too high, it will draw the visitor's eye up to the ceiling, probably not the most attractive part of the room. If hung too low, the same problem occurs except the eye will be lead to look at the floor and the room will seem low, underfoot and bottom heavy.

- Determine what 'eye-level' is by holding the picture where you think it should go and then lowering it a few inches. What you have found is that perfect, slightly above eye-level spot. The measurement in approximately 5' from the floor.

- Hanging a picture, or group of pictures, just slightly above eye-level will keep the mid-point of the room balanced. The floor and the ceiling will feel like they are evenly spaced apart from any place you stand in a room.

The room will be comfortable to those who enter it and the dimensions of the space will flow together. It can make or break the design of the room. As in marketing, the most expensive items are usually placed on shelves that are at your eye-level. Think of the cereal aisle in the commissary or supermarket; the top row is filled with natural grain and "adult" or "healthy" choices, perfectly located for grown-ups to see. The bottom row contains the children's "healthy" choices,, too low to even be recognized and that row right in the middle, exactly lined up to your child's eyeballs, are the brightly colored boxes, usually depicting popular characters and offering trendy prizes. It's the first thing their eye sees, nothing else in the aisle even matters.

- Too much or too little artwork in a room can directly affect the room's overall appearance. If the wall is large, the picture should be large, or there should be a group of pictures filling a large space. If the wall is small, then it could either remain empty or support one small photo or accent item. Hanging too many things on the same wall is not attractive. Each wall should have only one focal point of art. Be sure the space around the picture is remains clear so it the art is highlighted.
- When choosing frames for your pictures, try to keep them similar. Not matching necessarily, but similar in color and the material they are made of. Do not mix silver and gold with wood. Keep photos with photos and prints with prints. The closer the relationship, the more they will complement one another. Frameless frames are ideal when you are hanging a group of photographs. The focus will be on the pictures and not on the frames.

The same concept applies with the items used to adorn your living space. Your main focal elements should be at eye-level, like flower arrangements, mantle pieces and especially pictures.

So, how do you decide where to hammer in the first nail?

Figure out the placement and arrangement of the furniture in the room. Imagine you are your own guest, entering the room for the first time. Sounds silly, I know, but it works. What wall do you see upon entry, where does your eye jump? Sit on the furniture and notice what wall you are looking towards. These initial focal points are where your most important wall hangings should be hung.

To ensure accurate and fool-proof placement of wall hangings the first time, here is the best trick out there.

Tools Needed:
- Plain paper, large enough to trace your wall hanging (an open brown grocery bag works well)
- Pencil / pen
- Scissors
- Hammer
- Picture hanging nails, be sure they will support the weight of what you are hanging
- Scotch tape / masking tape

Steps to perfectly placed wall hangings:
- ❖ Get a roll of white paper, brown packing paper or even a few brown grocery bags.
- ❖ Lay your print or picture on the paper and, using a pencil, trace the frame.

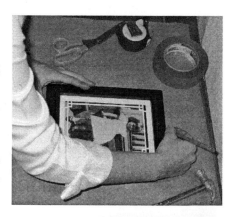

- ❖ Mark the front of the paper with a star or the word "FRONT". Turn the frame over, not the paper.

- ❖ Cut the paper on the lines so it is the same dimension as the frame that is being hung.

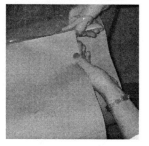

❖ Measure out where the nail should go in relation to the hanging hardware on the back of the frame. It should be in the center. If the hanging hardware is a wire, put tension on the wire and measure the hanging point from the top of the frame, mark the same measurement(s) onto the paper cutout. If there are more than two pieces of hanging hardware, mark them both on the paper.

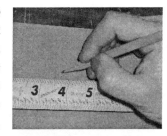

❖ Use tape to temporarily hang the paper cutout where you think the picture will be hung.

❖ Go back and sit on the furniture. Enter the room from each direction to be sure the picture can be seen from the different points of view and it is not blocked.

❖ Move the paper or pieces of paper around the room until you decide which placement is the best.

❖ Line up the nails with the markings on the paper. Hammer your nails into the wall. No need to remove the paper to do this step. Leave the paper hanging and hammer the nail right through.

❖ Once the nail is secure, remove the paper and replace it with your frame. Tah-Dah!

If you are hanging multiple frames in a row or identical photo frames or prints in a collage format, use the same technique. This allows you to play with the placement of the frames before actually hanging them.

Hanging pictures with identically sized frames normally requires the use of a level line. You can purchase a small level from a hardware store for a few dollars. If you do not have a level, you can double-check your placement by taping up the paper and measuring from the floor to the top of the paper. Don't measure from the ceiling. Floors are constructed and installed by contractors using a level. It is likely that a floor is more level than the ceiling.

That's a Wrap!

You should be very proud of yourself and all of the hard work you have put into turning 'That Military House' into 'Your Military Home'.

Your quarters are beginning to take shape, your clutter is reduced and your household is running like a finely tuned instrument. Your time is more manageable, schedules are less hassled and you actually have time for yourself to relax. What a wonderful feeling of success!

The hardest part is over and now you can sit back and enjoy the space around you. Remember that this new lifestyle must be maintained. Continue to practice the '**3-Box-Method**' of organizing and experiment with what you have each and every time you relocate and decorate your new home.

Keep your PCS, your Positive Change of Surroundings, as a fun and exciting time for you and your family to enjoy. Begin your relocation totally prepared, fully organized and completely open-minded and you will be ready for any journey your military career has in store.

Inventory Number Grid

1	2	3	4	5	6	7	8	9	10	11	12	13	14	15	16	17	18	19	20
21	22	23	24	25	26	27	28	29	30	31	32	33	34	35	36	37	38	39	40
41	42	43	44	45	46	47	48	49	50	51	52	53	54	55	56	57	58	59	60
61	62	63	64	65	66	67	68	69	70	71	72	73	74	75	76	77	78	79	80
81	82	83	84	85	86	87	88	89	90	91	92	93	94	95	96	97	98	99	100
101	102	103	104	105	106	107	108	109	110	111	112	113	114	115	116	117	118	119	120
121	122	123	124	125	126	127	128	129	130	131	132	133	134	135	136	137	138	139	140
141	142	143	144	145	146	147	148	149	150	151	152	153	154	155	156	157	158	159	160
161	162	163	164	165	166	167	168	169	170	171	172	173	174	175	176	177	178	179	180
181	182	183	184	185	186	187	188	189	190	191	192	193	194	195	196	197	198	199	200
201	202	203	204	205	206	207	208	209	210	211	212	213	214	215	216	217	218	219	220
221	222	223	224	225	226	227	228	229	230	231	232	233	234	235	236	237	238	239	240
241	242	243	244	245	246	247	248	249	250	251	252	253	254	255	256	257	258	259	260
261	262	263	264	265	266	267	268	269	270	271	272	273	274	275	276	277	278	279	280
281	282	283	284	285	286	287	288	289	290	291	292	293	294	295	296	297	298	299	300
301	302	303	304	305	306	307	308	309	310	311	312	313	314	315	316	317	318	319	320
321	322	323	324	325	326	327	328	329	330	331	332	333	334	335	336	337	338	339	340
341	342	343	344	345	346	347	348	349	350	351	352	353	354	355	356	357	358	359	360
361	362	363	364	365	366	367	368	369	370	371	372	373	374	375	376	377	378	379	380
381	382	383	384	385	386	387	388	389	390	391	392	393	394	395	396	397	398	399	400

Household Inventory Sheets

Room:

Item	Make	Model	Purchase Date	Cost	Receipt/Warrantee

Room:

Item	Make	Model	Purchase Date	Cost	Receipt/Warrantee

Room:

Item	Make	Model	Purchase Date	Cost	Receipt/Warrantee

Room:

Item	Make	Model	Purchase Date	Cost	Receipt/Warrantee

Room:

Item	Make	Model	Purchase Date	Cost	Receipt/Warrantee

Room:

Item	Make	Model	Purchase Date	Cost	Receipt/Warrantee

Room:

Item	Make	Model	Purchase Date	Cost	Receipt/Warrantee

Room:

Item	Make	Model	Purchase Date	Cost	Receipt/Warrantee

About the Author
Sandee Payne

Born and raised in Audubon, New Jersey, Sandee's family household was always buzzing with creativity. Her mother's love for crafting and sewing, combined with her father's passions in woodworking and graphic design, have all found their way into Sandee's forte.

This pioneering new author is known in many military communities today as "Sandee Payne", usually spoken as one word. Sandee has been an active duty Army spouse for 10 years. Relocating her family many times, to follow her husband Michael's career, she has become accustomed to the many changing that must take place in the home every time there is a move.

Sandee has been freelancing her knowledge and expertise regarding decorating and organizing with families and friends at every installation in which her family has been stationed, including Ft. Drum, NY, Ft. Leonard Wood, MO, three consecutive tours in Germany counting Vilseck, Bamberg and Wurzburg and Newport, RI. From teaching decorating classes at conferences and workshops to renovating and redecorating government quarters, private residences and military facilities, Sandee has gotten her hands on it all.

She now has taken those experiences, references and professional knowledge to collectively and creatively designed this 'how-to' guide for moving Military families.

'That Military House: Move it, Organize it & Decorate it', will inspire you with tips, techniques and ideas that will surely improve the way your house looks, feels and functions, no matter where it is you call "home".

References

Eiseman, Leartice. Colors For Your Every Mood: Discover Your True Decorating Colors., Copyright 1998 by Leatrice Eiseman. Published by Capital Books, Inc. Sterling, Virginia.

Hansgen, Karen. The Nook Book., Copyright 2003 and Published by Clarkson Potter/Publishing, New York, New York.

Martha Stewart Living: Simple Home Solutions., Copyright 2004 by Martha Stewart Living Omnimedia, Inc. Published by Clarkson Potter/Publishers, New York, New York.

Morgenstern, Julie. Organizing from the Inside Out., Copyright 1998 by Julie Morgenstern. Published by Henry Holt and Company, LLC, New York, New York.

Reader's Digest Complete Book of Home Decorating., Copyright 2001 by Eaglemoss Publications Ltd., Published by Reader's Digest.

Ward, Lauri. Use What You Have Decorating. Copyright 1998 by Lauri Ward. Published by G. P. Putnam's Sons. New York, New York.

Webster, Richard. Feng Shui for Beginners: Successful Living by Design., Copyright 1997 by Richard Webster. Published by Llewellyn Publications, St. Paul, Minnesota.

Wolfman, Peri and Charles Gold. A Place for Everything: Organizing the Stuff of Life., Copyright 1999 by Peri Wolfman and Charles Gold. Published by Clarkson Potter/Publishers, New York, New York.

Product Resources

Ballard Designs:	ballarddesigns.com
Bed Bath & Beyond:	bedbathandbeyond.com
Brother:	brother.com
Claires:	claires.com
Country Curtains:	countrycurtains.com
Crate & Barrel:	crateandbarrel.com
HaBa:	haba.com
Hallmark:	hallmark.com
Hold Everything:	holdeverything.com
i Room Dividers:	ikea.com
Ikea:	iroomdividers.com
JC Penney:	jcpenney.com
Kitchenaide:	kitchenaide.com
Linens-N-Things:	lnt.com
MoMA Store:	momastore.com
Overstock:	overstock.com
Patina Stores:	patinastores.com
Pier 1 Imports:	pier1.com
Pottery Barn:	potterybarn.com
Restoration Hardware:	restorationhardware.com
Rubbermaid:	rubbermaid.com
Sherwin Williams:	sherwin-williams.com
Storehouse:	storehouse.com
Target:	target.com
The Company Store:	thecontainerstore.com
The Container Store:	thecompanystore.com
The Home Depot:	homedepot.com
Lowes	lowes.com

Graphic Resources

www.1contemporary.com
www.3m.com
www.amgmedia.com
www.antiquescientifica.com
www.anythinganimals.com
www.artlab.com
www.avm.com
www.battleduck.com
www.bbc.co.uk
www.bhg.com
www.cableorganizer.com
www.charlevoixantiques.com
www.classicradiators.co.uk
www.comfortzonebaby.com
www.compusa.com
www.containers-bins-boxes-shelving.com
www.creativespacesonline.com
www.cs.odu.edu
www.ddcnyc.com
www.digsmagazine.com
www.dro.com
www.drugstore.com
www.familyfun.com
www.fashion-era.com
www.wallwords.com

www.fromoldbooks.org
www.gardianoffers.co.uk
www.homedecorators.com
www.hormel.com
www.houarth-timber.co.uk
www.italianartstore.com
www.kidsquartersonline.com
www.larstetens.com
www.minidiscaccess.com
www.naturesflavors.com
www.oldporthomes.com
www.outletcomputerfurniture.com
www.realestate.com
www.scrippscollege.edu
www.shawnafeeley.com
www.simplyorganized.com
www.soleberry.com
www.sptimes.com
www.sw-asia.com
www.thewhiteco.com
www.tv-sets.com
www.ufofabrics.com
www.vandykes.com
www.xenographia.com
www.wisegeek.com

Visit us online today!

www.thatmilitaryhouse.com

Register on-line and receive
Updates, Promotions and Newsletters
from:

That Military House
Move it
organize it
&
Decorate it

Contact the author:
info@thatmilitaryhouse.com

Bulk Sales and Retail Distribution:
sales@thatmilitaryhouse.com